Contents

List of Figures

Acknowledgments

To my parents, I owe all that I have become. My father, Oscar Jr., taught me not only what it means to be a man, but also what it means to be a Freemason. His deeds were his true secrets. In times of strife, he took the high road. He exemplified Freemasonic principles and teachings not just in the Lodge, but in his daily life. He treated all upon the level and he acted upon the square. He was born at the end of World War I, came of age during the great depression, and enlisted in the U.S. Navy during World War II. He served his community as a policeman for more than thirty-five years both before and after the war while working side jobs as a carpenter, mechanic, and, even, a NASCAR owner and driver. He was made a Freemason prior to World War II and faithfully served the Craft for more than sixty-five years. If I am half the man he was, I will be well satisfied.

My mother, Frances, taught me tolerance and concern for my fellow man. She was a compassionate lady who displayed every day grace and kindness. Born one of nine children at the beginning of World War I, she also came of age during the great depression. And although she remained on the home front during World War II, she faithfully served as a telephone operator and making cloth for military uniforms. She counseled me when needed, guided me on the right path, supported me always, and lovingly forgave me when necessary.

My grandmother, Daisy, taught me to love literature and gave me an in-depth knowledge of *The Bible*. She was a true southern lady in the finest sense. As a teenager before the end of the nineteenth century, she was privileged to attend "finishing school" where she became an aspiring poet and tennis player. She continued to write throughout her life, though she never published. She taught me that aspirations were important and that no matter where your roots lay or what adversities confronted you, your achievements are limited only by your imagination and your dedication.

My grandfather, Oscar Sr., gave me a strong work ethic and aided with my spirituality. He was an "old school" Methodist in the strict sense, yet he taught me compassion and understanding. He treated all people as his equal regardless of race or religion. He was a carpenter, black smith, and mechanic. He taught me how to use tools, lay a foundation, raise a wall, plumb and level, and finish my labor in a timely manner at a marked level of distinction. The houses he built still stand while others have dissolved into dust and ruin. His legacy is those who came after him.

My high school teachers, especially in math and English, as well as several college mentors encouraged me to attain at the highest level and assured me that education was the key to self-improvement. In the military, especially in combat, I encountered many dedicated noncommissioned and commissioned officers who gave me guidance and counsel, and who, in later years, supported me when I stepped into what was for me "unknown territory." My graduate school mentors and advisors encouraged me to become a professor and to research and write, informing me that my diligence would be rewarded. And the academic administrators who invited me to work at their universities before and after I became an administrator myself gave me sound guidance in professionalism, organization, and supervision as well as an education in how to motivate and lead a most diverse population.

And never to be forgotten are those myriad students who passed through my classes during those thirty-five years, with many of whom I remain in contact. They remind me often through their successes that in some way I had a positive impact on their lives. The greatest praise I have received is from a former student who is of a different faith and background who wrote to me that I had a significant positive impact on his ethical decision making process for which he would be forever thankful.

To my Masonic brethren, I thank them for their fellowship, guidance, and support. When I came to the Fraternity, I expected friendship, but not to the extent received. I looked for Masonic education and found a wealth of information available. In turn, I learned that I had something to contribute and was encouraged to do so. I could instruct and have now taught many catechism classes, mentoring as we learned. One student is now Worshipful Master of my Lodge and others are "in line."

I express my deepest fraternal thanks to the members of my Lodge and Grand Lodge who encouraged me to "enter into the line" and to serve my Grand Lodge in Masonic Education as well as Public Education and Citizenship. Their support and their brotherly love is without measure. R∴W∴ Troy Usina quietly encouraged me to pursue a Masonic career by appointing me as a District Committeeman and M∴W∴Jorge Aladro encouraged me further by appointing me to a State Chairmanship. M∴W∴ Robert Harry has been a constant mentor. There are so many others who have motivated me to progress, but I am especially grateful to W∴James Davis and Bro. David Pierucci for their support, guidance, and lively conversation.

I am also deeply appreciative of time and effort taken by M∴W∴Robert Harry and Jorge Aladro for their close reading of the manuscript and their comments and suggestion which served to strengthen this book. Their assistance was invaluable.

Finally, and above all, to my wife Julie—my constant friend, companion, and love of my live. She has stood by me through trials, troubles, and difficulties, as well as joy and exhilaration, and has gracefully assumed the role of a "Masonic Widow," I can only offer my deepest and most profound love, commitment, and thanks. Without her, this book would not have come to fruition. She told me "you have something to say, write it." And she granted me the time necessary to see the project to fruition. Forever and always.

Introduction

The study of ritual has emerged over the past thirty years as a sound field for philosophical, academic, and theological discourse. Ritual is a living thing and is neither a "cookie cutter" exercise nor a set of timeless practices fit only for curious observation and imitation in the modern world. It is a complex system of cultural constructions, traditions, self-expressions, theology transmitted esoterically, and symbolism. It is capable of transmitting through words and actions which include a variety of role models, the rich density of human life.

"The meaning of ritual is deep indeed" wrote Xunzi in the third century B.C.E. It is a great and lofty enterprise and those who try to enter "with the violent and arrogant ways of those who despise common customs and consider themselves to be above other men will meet his downfall there."

This text endeavors to briefly address the depth of the ritualistic experience through an historical and psychological analysis of ritual dynamics—what ritual means to man as well as what man means to ritual. The expression of thought through the duality of action and words is addressed, as well as is the psychological impact of ritual and the physiological implications of its practice. Ritual is human behavior at its most perfect. It is spiritual, rational, and cultural.

Ritual is not the direct result of any one human action or train of thought. And as noted in Chapter IV, the question of which came first, ritual or community is yet to be answered. Ritual is much talked about yet little understood, possibly because the modern world tends to downplay the possibility that humans are affected by what they see and hear.

Ritual teaches us about reality but we will not come to a full understanding of it if we disparage what others do and view their actions from a pseudo-position of intellectual and cultural superiority. Ritual is, writes Catherine

Bell, is an interaction of body and mind which "by virtue of movement and stillness, sound and silence" enables humans to experience and interpret events. It establishes levels of professionalism as it generates and transmits traditions.

Yet ritual is something that can be taught. Rituals are repetitive and rhythmic which contribute to their ready retention and transmission. They come in all sizes and link humans in a multitude of ways. Ritual is expressed in architecture as well as performance. It is not empty or hollow, but when properly performed in an appropriate environment directly effects the human psyche in ways no other event can achieve.

Ritual is at the core of Freemasonry and is that thing which sets us apart from so many social and fraternal organizations. It is the key to our "secrets" and the manner through which we transmit our "beautiful system of morality." It is something to be treasured, maintained, taught, elevated, evaluated, and, above, reinforced through proper performance, decorum, and setting.

Chapter One

Ritual Light

Repetition and familiarity work. What is repeated becomes familiar, and this becomes a part of us. Our own culture understands this . . . ritual has always been and will always be a means of securing for future generations the power and reality of the Gospel.
—Peter Enns, *Exodus: The NIV Application Commentary*

Figure 1.1.   Ritual 1.

The study of ritual as a discrete cultural and human phenomenon is relatively new, emerging only in the late 1970s and early 1980s. It draws from earlier and current research in the fields of anthropology, sociology, history, ethology, and religion. Ritual is one of the basic elements that make us human. It is evolutionary in nature and is a fundamental feature of all human and animal

1

behavior. It is something we cannot do without and it is impossible to avoid. It is biological and psychological as well as spiritual. It requires time, effort, skill, dedication, study, practice, energy, repetition, and, yes, even money. We may not consider ourselves ritual creatures, but our society is permeated with weddings, funerals, parades, graduations, inaugurations, and a wide variety of rites of passage, all of which are ritualistic in nature. When we explore the nature of ritual, we explore also its place, power, and its potential for transformation in self and society.

Ritual is founded on beliefs that are secure against the intrusion of other social constructs. At the same time, ritual has an integral role in the production of those beliefs. Ritual is about belonging and includes attraction, identification, and group cohesion. While all group membership arises from a combination of choice, chance, and opportunity, once a member, the very nature of human social interdependence results in a potent, secure belonging often established through ritual. Belonging to a group is regularly accompanied by transitions. In Freemasonry these transitions are demonstrated through the three Degrees of the Symbolic Lodge as well as through initiation or reception into various appendant bodies. As one moves forward or transitions, relationships change; old ones are relaxed and new ones formed. Paramount to this experience in the Craft is *communitas*—the developing of a cohort that bonds Brothers. Ritual is fundamental to this process.

Ritual is found in all cultures and is as innate a part of modern industrialized society as it is of tribal society. The term "ritual" is no longer a lighting-rod for suspicion and is now understood and studied as a significant social phenomenon. Early studies of ritual often deemed it only as conformity to community and thus ignored the strong contributions ritual makes in modern society. Its study was often considered unnecessary because those who engaged in it were deemed lacking in academic credentials and the studies devoid of "hard" research. Ritual was too often considered an art worthy only of observation, not a human experience requiring research and analysis. "The arts can look after themselves; they are used to neglect and obfuscation"[1] was the generally held opinion. In the film version of Evelyn Waugh's *Brideshead Revisited*, these words are put into the mouth of Charles Ryder when asked by Markaster about art: "What do you want to be an artist for? I mean, what's the point of it? Why don't you just buy a bloody camera and take a bloody photograph and stop giving yourself airs? That's what I want to know." Ryder responds by saying "Because, a camera is a mechanical device which records a moment in time, but not what that moment means or the emotions that it evokes. Whereas, a painting, however imperfect it may be, is an expression of feeling. An expression of love. Not just a copy of something."[2] This is ritual as well, it is not a copy; it is an expression of an emotion and, though often imperfect, is, as Waugh notes, a manifestation of feeling and brotherly love.

Ritual appears to be external and group oriented, yet individual philosophy and identity contribute greatly to its understanding and impact. This leads to the study of ritual in both *epistemological* and *metaphysical* terms. Epistemology refers to our knowledge of ritual methods and includes a determination of the performance as ritual as opposed to simple repetitive behavior as well as a determination of where the ritual begins and ends. A metaphysical analysis of ritual focuses on and answers questions such as "what makes a performance a ritual?" and "what parts make it a proper ritual?" While the metaphysical study of ritual presents problems for many scholars based upon an assumption that all ritual study is descriptive rather than scientific or, even, theological, when ritual is classified as an individual activity resulting in change, its study is greatly facilitated.

Ritual is truly transformative and leads to change, both to the individual and, over time, to the ritual. It is a mirror of society and a model for transition. As Catherine Bell notes in *Ritual: Perspectives and Dimensions*, there were significant changes made in Christian ritual from the time of the early church (second to fourth century) through and beyond the Reformation which resulted in "a constant diet of dramatic upheavals and gradual modifications."[3] And these changes in Christian ritual are ongoing as witnessed in developments in modern mega churches and non-denominationalism. Freemasonry has been no different. The ceremonies engaged in by our ancient brothers during the operative centuries (eleventh through the sixteenth) were most likely simple initiations into a craft during which the apprentice pledged allegiance to the guild, to the church, and to the government. After which he was rewarded with "words" and "signs" that would enable him to engage in his trade wherever he might travel.

As Freemasonry transformed from an operative guild based on the knowledge of the skilled workman to a speculative society seeking knowledge about the higher activities of man, the ritual of initiation and, later, advancement, transformed to meet the new nature of the Craft. Elias Ashmole wrote in his diary on 16 October 1646: "4:30 p.m., I was made a Free-Mason at Warrington in Lancashire with Col. Henry Mainwaring of Karincham in Cheshire."[4] He then lists the names of those in attendance but he gives no details about the actual ceremony. Typical of Freemasonry and of Masonic minutes, little information is available about these early rituals. Some inferences may be made, however, from the records that do survive.

Prior to about 1725, no reference can be found to three separate degrees in Freemasonry. The terms most commonly used were "Making a Brother" or "Making a Free Mason." All candidates were simply "entered." A man asked a Masonic friend to be allowed to join the lodge. His qualifications were openly debated in the Lodge at some length with his proposer serving as his advocate and the Brothers present as the examiners. The candidate, of course, was not present which required that the proposer be very familiar with the candidate, his record, his family, his history, and the benefit associated with admitting him into the Lodge. His name was then put to a secret vote—the ballot—with a single dissent sufficient for rejection. If he was approved, he was sent a written summons informing him to appear with his proposer at a specified place on a given date. There was no waiting for investigation. It was assumed that if a Brother of a Lodge recommended a man for membership, he knew the candidate very well and personally, and was positive that his record would survive the test of open debate in the lodge. Brethren at that time would never have considered proposing someone whom they did not know and know well.

On the day of the initiation, usually late afternoon as Ashmole notes, the Lodge was opened with the Master asking if anyone was in waiting to be "made a Mason." The Wardens and proposer prepared the candidate—divested of minerals and metals, and so forth—and he was asked some basic questions similar to the modern Senior Deacon's anteroom lecture. The Wardens returned to the Lodge while the candidate and his proposer waited in complete silence in the totally dark anteroom for at least thirty minutes. At some later point, this waiting period became the Chamber of Reflection.

Since Lodges had no permanent home, a set of figures was drawn on the floor within an oblong square (usually on the second floor or upper room) with charcoal or chalk. Masonic symbols were added and a tracing board put in place near the Master's station. The proposer then brought the candidate into the lodge "upon the point of a sword or spear" in the small of the back and, in later generations, led by a Deacon with a sword. Prayer may have been offered based upon the tradition of that Lodge. Moderns tended to omit the prayer upon admission while Ancients (Antients) included it. The circumambulation followed which presented the Brother-to-be to the members present. He was then led to the altar and given the obligation which, since it was only one degree, included most of the penalties in the modern first and second degrees. The candidate was required to obligate himself on the Volume of Sacred Law declaring that he would preserve the *mysteries* not the just secrets of the craft. The words and signs of recognition were communicated to him by his proposer or, possibly, the Master, who then asked him to demonstrate his proficiency for all present. A charge was given informing the new Brother of his duty to God, his master, his nation, his craft, and his fellow men. A history of the craft, usually taken from one of several ancient documents such as the *Regius Manuscript* or poem, the *Cooke Manuscript*, or *Grand Lodge Manuscript No. 1,* was read or, possibly, recited to the new Brother. These early charges or histories varied markedly in their accounts of the Craft's history with the Legend of Hiram totally absent. Instead, we find the Legend of Noah as mentioned in the *Regius* poem (abt. 1390) with longer versions of the story found in the *Cooke Manu-*

script of 1410 and the *Graham Manuscript* of the early 1700s (see Chapter VII).

With the trestle or feasting board already in place, the pattern on the floor and the emblems on the tracing board were explained (the modern version of this part of the ritual is the lecture). The new brother was then instructed to "wash away" the figures on the floor, retire to the preparation room, recover his valuables, and return to the lodge. Upon his return, he was presented with a white leather apron and its meaning explained. The craft then assembled in a circle, hands joined crossways to form a chain, and the ceremony was ended. The Lodge was finally closed when the Senior Warden said "Our Master's will and pleasure is that this Lodge stands closed till" after which he would give the date and time of the next meeting. A more complete description of this process is to be found in Chapter VIII.

The ritual described above is significantly different from the modern three-degree system found in most Blue Lodges. The evolution from a single "making" ceremony to three discrete degrees is a reflection of the theory of individualism in ritual practice and of innovation over time. The three-degree system was the result of intense reflection over at least a century and a half, and demonstrated the desire of Freemasons to more fully educate the Brethren about the mysteries, history, and philosophy of the Craft. By the 1840s, however, the "pendulum swung" in the United States away from measured advancement and philosophical/moral instruction to quicker advancement and national conformity.

This change or innovation was led in the United States by Masonic Brothers, thinkers, ritualists, and writers in reaction to the wave of anti-Masonry that followed the Second Great Awakening which began about 1790 but reached its height after 1824. The Second Great Awakening found its center in the "burned-over" district of New York. Its prime proponent was Charles Finney, an itinerant evangelist. The geographical center of the movement was Genesee County and its county seat, Batavia. In addition, the Anti-Masonic Party, a one issue-party founded in 1828 and later merged with the Whig Party, gave political support to the cause. It became obvious to Freemasons that their very existence was threatened and they sought to relieve external pressures by making internal changes. By the early 1840s, there was also a desire for some type of national uniformity of work as expressed at two National Masonic Conventions. The first one was held in Washington, DC, in 1842 and the second in Baltimore in 1843. The result of those conferences was a "recommendation" to bar Entered Apprentices and Fellow Crafts from participating in regular Lodge meetings to enhance security. This resulted in the abandonment of the thoughtful developmental system previously used which led the Brother through the three degrees over a marked period of time and provided significant opportunity for education and discussion, and replacing it with more simple memorization, rote catechisms, and formal

ᴐ   e possible doing all Lodge business in the most advanced
many Brethren present as possible. Yet, as late as 1852, Dr.
tchel, Past Grand Master of Missouri, wrote in *The Masonic*
_____ ary Mirror that "various schemes and devices and non-essen-
tial changes were proposed, among which it was gravely suggested that all
members of Lodges must be M.Ms.. In some Jurisdictions this system was
adopted, in others, the *good old way was adhered to"* [emphasis added].⁵
The attitude of individual Brothers, Lodges, and Grand Lodges about the
adoption of new ritual, whatever the reasoning, reflects the paradox of our
Anglo-Saxon tradition of democratic action: the consent of the Brethren is
required, and but not always given.

Ritual is not strictly the arcane domain of parish priests, shamans, or
Freemasons. Ritual is not confined to a specific place or time, nor is it always
defined by a specific compact or relationship between actor and event. It
arises out of ordinary business life as well as an expression of devotion to
Deity. Masonic ritual arose out of the business practice of obligating an
apprentice to a term of service and the necessity of maintaining trade secrets.
We are, as humans, inveterate ritualizers. We find fulfillment in linking the
mythic and symbolic with our daily lives. We seek, through ritual, to answer
questions about ultimateness, awe, eternity, involvement, and the human
experience. Ritual provides a means for decoding, interpreting, and internal-
izing everyday events. The symbols of ritual create a tapestry of our political,
social, artistic, intellectual, and spiritual lives. It is the means by which we
transmit from generation to generation the symbolism of our culture with
their valuable storehouse of information as well as rules for governing that
information. Ritual, notes Peter McLaren, is "the pivot of the world . . . the
foundation of institutional life . . . the essential constitution of classroom
life."⁶

Ritual is not, however, entropic gestural noise accompanied by random
motions which lack predictability, syntax, and patterns of meaning. Ritual is
"not sporadic, compulsive," nor lacking in rhythm or meaningful gestures.⁷ It
possesses the capacity to *point beyond* the symbol so that the meaning becomes greater than the gestures, words, or the ritual itself.

Ritual has been studied, at some level, as a forceful cultural experience
for at least one hundred and fifty years though originally in its relation to
theology and drama rather than as a philosophical, psychological, and
physiological phenomenon. It is more than a tool for understanding social
occurrences and dramatizations; it is a window into the human experience.
Ritual influences both social cohesion and equilibrium, and, through experience and performance, it contributes directly to understanding. It facilitates
the integration of belief and behavior; tradition and change; the real and the
ideal. But ritual is, above all, doing. Just like swimming, riding a bike, or
engaging in sports, we learn about ritual by doing it. And once we have

mastered the doing, we take the next logical steps and begin to think, read, write, and theorize about the process. At this point, our thinking about ritual moves beyond the physical to the sublime and our ideas about it are shaped by the text as well as the experience.

Virtually all sacred texts contain a number of descriptions detailing how rituals are to be performed, but these texts also contain critical reflection on the value of rituals in terms of social cohesion and moral meaning. The great Confucian texts, for example, provide an abundance of information about the relationship between religious ritual and social harmony. And the Hebrew *Bible* often discusses ritual in moral as well as societal terms. Even Chaucer's *Canterbury Tales*, which describes in such vivid imagery a fictional pilgrimage beginning at the Tabard Inn outside London and ending in Canterbury at the shrine of St. Thomas Beckett, is ritualistic in form in that it is the tale of a journey. Masonic ritual is of the same format: the recounting of a physical and intellectual journey.

While ritual is most often associated with religion and studied as a sacred act, culturally speaking, it is much more. Ritual is language, reason, and the use of symbols and tools that distinguishes humans from other animals. A great deal of ritual theory arose from the field of ethology or the detailed observation of animal behavior, but such study often resulted in what Barry Stephenson refers to as kind of circular thinking in that it is *human* behavior that allows ethologists to perceive animal behavior as an expression of ritual. The difference between animal and human behavior is that humans possess the ability to evaluate and criticize their performance outside the ultimate result of the ritual, something that is absent in the animal world. Animals do not analyze nor do they correct instinctive rituals. Only humans are capable of reflection, evaluation, and change. For example, there is a deep-seated fear in many cultures and religions that mistakes in ritual will have real-world results thus necessitating extensive practice accompanied by ongoing reflection and change to address the minutest perceived error. In some cultures, there are even rituals specifically designed to correct all errors in ritual of the previous year, observed and unobserved, known and unknown. Essentially, incorrect performance equates with non-performance and the impact of the ritual is nullified.

The majority of formal ritual involves participants engaging in acts to which they may not assign specific meaning. They are using what they learned—in theatre it might be called "blocking"—to communicate meaning to the other participants and to the audience. They are acting a part without necessarily experiencing a direct emotional connection to the character. This is ritual in its most prescribed and invariant form. And despite the fact that modern industrialization and communication technologies have created a world vastly different from that of Stonehenge or early sixteenth century England, ritual is as integral a part of contemporary life as it was in the lives of our ancestors. Rituals are more than what Peter McLaren described as purely cosmetic: they are not mere trappings or even toys to be manipulated by sociological theorists. Rituals speak directly to the very nature of what it means to be human and they play a role in both our biological and cultural development.

All humans participate in ritualistic behavior. The question is "why?" While the earliest attempts to explain rituals were couched in their association with lofty endeavors and the sacred, further study has demonstrated that human rituals are part of everyday, run-of-the mill life and their explanations are to be found in the community, not the heavens. Human behavior is far less instinctive (God given, if you will) than animal behavior. We proceed through our lives not merely driven by our biology, but rather by utilizing a wide range of communication behaviors which constitute culture. Humans are capable of ideation—the capacity to hold beliefs—and moralization—the ability to assign good and bad intentions to an action. Humans are also capable of forming opinions, attitudes, and beliefs which guide their behavior. The question, however, is which came first, ritual or ideation/moralization? Roy Rappaport in *Ritual and Religion in the Making of Humanity* argues that many human endeavors were prompted by ritual but were not their origin.

Ritual, in this dimension, is a template for behavior. For example, there is no doubt that humans have engaged in some form of warfare from the beginnings of the species but open warfare is expensive in terms of commodities and human life. Many ritual theorists suggest that humans adopted ritualized warfare to replace the terrible toll of the actual thing and that this form of warfare morphed, at points, into ceremony and performance. For example, Edward I of England (1239-1307) participated in a tournament or joust specifically arranged on his behalf in June 1256. Tournaments were highly ritualized events which provided young knights the opportunity to demonstrate their skills and introduce them to the "law of chivalry." Tournaments did now always replace warfare, but they did provide an energetic outlet for those involved and may have served to reduce internecine conflict. They also, and more importantly, resulted in far less injury and loss of life, and required significantly less expenditure of time, energy, and national wealth.

The tournaments of the early thirteenth century had little resemblance to those of later generations, however, when spectacle trumped performance. The tournaments of Edward's time were mock battles staged over a wide area in which two teams endeavored to outmaneuver and capture the opponent. They were very similar to modern military and industrial team-building exercises. An important part of these exercises were taunts and insults, but they also provided an opportunity to correct mistakes, characterize misdeeds, and correct wrongs without depending upon actual warfare to provide the teaching tools, and they served to instill in participants and spectators the essential elements of the chivalric tradition.

The utilization of ritual to address conflict and aggression as well as issues of morality and virtue is a social control mechanism. "Rites of rebellion," as Max Gluckman calls them, allows the conflict to be acted out without harm to the participants and serves as a teaching tool that provides for the maintenance of civil society. Warfare is a significant step up from ritualized violence and is destructive both to the individual and to the group, thus to be avoided. In non-industrialized cultures and among indigenous peoples, warfare itself is highly ritualized thus resulting in relatively harmless conflict when compared to the chaotic, non-ritualized warfare engaged in by modern, industrial nations.

A significant amount of human behavior can then be explained and comprehended in terms of rituals which involve communication, meaning, and understanding, and which teach valuable lessons about life and community. This leads directly to the consideration of the role and purpose of ritual in society. We did not first evolve as humans and then, at some point, decide to perform rituals. Ritualization, modern scholars suggests, is part of our biological and cultural evolution. The first evidence of ritual, noted Werner Herzog in 2010 his film *Cave of the Forgotten Dreams*, is the Chauvet-Pont-d'Arc Caves in southern France which were decorated some 30,000 to 32,000 years ago. More recent research suggests that human expressions of creativity, which is inherent to ritual, may extend back more than 165,000 years to Neanderthal stone circles with evidence of ritual sacrifice dating back some 65,000 to 70,000 years. Recently published archeological research provides a time and location line that indicates that some form of ritual activity was being performed not only in France, but also in Romania, Brazil, Australia, India, and Indonesia in the distant past. Not only is ritual, writes Stephenson, "something we do, it is often the subject of our imaginative lives, taken up in art, music, literature, and film"[8] and in Freemasonry, in our degree work.

Ritual, however, even within an organization such as a church or fraternity, is not static nor is it constant from location to location. This is probably the result of the use of symbolization in the ritual process. Ritual, notes Douglas Marshall, "requires symbolic content."[9] It is one of a handful of methods available to humans to produce belonging and group membership, and the use of physical sensation or symbolized physical sensation is one of the most effective means available to focus attention that results in a loss of self and the creation of concomitant group membership. Blood-wings is an initiation ritual suffered to some graduates of the United States Army Airborne School and the United States Army Air Assault School. And though rare, is usually presented by a superior to an elite soldier who has reached a significant career transition point. The superior would probably have received the same honor at his own graduation. The risky offer of blood wings to a transitioning soldier is considered an honor and the graduate nearly always has the option of rejecting the offer, and some do. For as in Freemasonry, it is the symbolism that counts, not the physical act.

One problem confronting the practice of ritual in the modern world is that there exists within many advanced cultures numerous alternative explanations for ritual effects. In order for ritual to achieve a marked level of belonging or other effect, it must be deemed scarce or difficult to obtain outside the ritual context itself. Ritual, then, is an effective force for both the creation of belief, but more importantly, for the establishment of a sense of "belonging."

When studying any human activity, and ritual is a human activity, one of the potential "traps" is propounding theories as facts. What, then, was the role of ritual in early culture? All answers are highly speculative yet through observation of the present—observation of current reality-- accompanied with an analysis of the historical record, we may generate rational scientific explanations for past ritual behavior and its contribution to the present. A theory is the explanation of an observation based on research and is open to further research and revision or rejection. Ritual is not, research suggests, an anachronistic remnant of our past that is of little use in the current enlightened age. Ritual has a purpose or function in society: it increases the likelihood of survival for the species or the organization. Ritual binds humans into groups thus facilitating their harmonious functioning. It maintains order and gives the group meaning, purpose, and value. Ritual has a definitive place in our social institutions, and as Joseph Campbell notes in *The Power of Myth* "If you want to find out what it means to have a society without rituals, read the New York *Times. . .* destructive and violent acts by young people who don't know how to behave in a civilized society." Bill Moyers responded: "Society has provided them no rituals by which they become members . . . of the community."[10]

Campbell also states that "This [Masonry] is a scholarly attempt to reconstruct an order of initiation that would result in spiritual revelation" with Moyers saying: "So when these men talked about the eye of God being reason, they were saying that the ground of our being as a society, as a culture, as a people, derives from the fundamental nature of the universe?" Campbell then replies: "That's what this first pyramid says. This is the pyramid of the world, and this is the pyramid of our society, and they are of the order. This is God's creation, and this is our society."[11] This order, this spiritual revelation is expressed through Masonic ritual.

Emil Durkheim writes that ritual is the method whereby individuals are brought together to "strengthen the bonds attaching the individual to the society of which he is a member."[12] It shapes our awareness of both the human and the divine as it socializes humans. Taylor, Robertson, Smith, and Frazer, note that the very nature of the act is intrinsic to how the ritual functions in society. [13] Ritual facilitates the means by which human beings live together in an orderly social relationship by maintaining the unity of the group. Ritual diffuses from generation to generation the basic attitudes of a society thus serving to "reduce anxiety, distress, fear, doubt, and, even, sorrow."[14] But, as Julian Huxley notes, the contemporary world fails to ritualize effectively which "leads to a high tendency toward flawed communication as well as a weakening of personal and social bonds."[15] How then, does ritual accomplish socialization?

Ritual begins with some form of experience which one or more members of the group wish to share with others, usually through symbolic means. Through this mutual sharing, Rappaport suggests, as well as the repetition of the ritual, a sense of permanence is attained with its accompanying reliability, certainty, perception of truth, and a shared experience of the world. Generally, the understanding and sharing of the experience that infuses ritual is not readily obtainable through other means. Ritual generally involves structure, order, and hierarchy that describe the human situation. And postmodern sentiments to the contrary, people desire to fully understand how their culture is structured and to engage in the *communitas* which results from the sharing of events. Ritual does not cloak or disharmonize social structures; rather it provides unity and harmony, and reduces the possibility of disruptive behavior.

Significant problems arise in the transmission of ritual with the lapse of time coupled with the natural forgetfulness of humankind. If a ritual is not repeated in a relatively short period, especially those of an esoteric nature which are not committed to paper or other storage systems, the scope and practices of the "old" traditions are often forgotten, misinterpreted, or misrepresented. When this happens, it becomes the domain of the current generation to reinvent or recover what was lost. The constant use of ritual, however, prevents this lapse and enhances the ritual experience by ensuring that all involved are fully aware of their connection to the past and their commitment to the future.

Ritual is as natural to humans as is walking and talking: and as crawling changes to walking and walking to running or, even, sprinting, so too does ritual change. Ritual promotes transformation in the individual and in the group, and along with deeper insight and the establishment of social order, serves to bind the participants into one band or fellowship. The power of ritual is most commonly found, scholars suggest, in initiation rites or rites of passage.

The Latin root for the word *initiation* literally means "beginning" or "entrance." An initiation ritual, therefore, changes an individual in some way. The priest is changed from a layman to a clergyman through ordination (initiation) as surely as the young teen was changed from a child under the care of his mother to an apprentice bound to his craft in medieval European guilds. Initiation is a "coming of age" during which the initiate learns respect

for elders, the history of the organization, and the skills or practical knowledge necessary to full participation in the group. Initiation ritual is not, however, a mere reenactment of set beliefs or even a narrative of past events. It is,
as noted, a time of transition and transformation. Ritual in this mode is a part
of the cycle of life, a sequential method, which, amidst its various steps and
ceremonies, takes the individual through a journey of time, space, and meaning.

How does ritual work? It works because we agree that it does. It is much
like the theatre or a movie: we willing suspend disbelief for a certain period
and agree that what we witnessed had an impact and that impact was the one
intended. As with hypnosis, ritual is a consent activity. It works because we
consent to having our mental categories and understanding of the world
reoriented in new ways through the symbolic composition of the ritual. Does
a ritual magically change an individual? No! Any change is a result of the
willingness to be changed and to an acceptance of the efficacy of the ritual as
a change agent.

A review of the vast literature concerning ritual emphasizes that it is a
variety of actions; that it is cultural; and that, as a medium, it has power.
Ritual includes a large grouping of human actions and beliefs to include
order, custom, morals, actions, worship, assembling, secret knowledge, separating, and gathering together, but more does not necessarily mean better.
Sometimes a minimalist approach to ritual is preferable. An overly extended
or intricate ritual may generate as much confusion as it does understanding,
and, over an extended period, ritual loses its psychological impact. To borrow from Aristotle, ritual should be neither excessive nor deficient. It should
display symmetry, proportion, and harmony. It should fit into the allotted
psychological time-frame.

Ritual is, above all, performance. It alters the physical world and "says"
things. It is symbolic communication in its highest form. The words used in
ritual not only provide information and background, they also facilitate transformation. When a priest or minister says "I now pronounce you husband and
wife," a transformation has taken place. Two singularities have become a
duality. But the words alone do not convey the full impact of the act. The
entire ceremony—the performance—does that. Ritual is thus a form of theatre that reinforces behavior—what Richard Schechner refers to as "twice
behaved behavior."[16] But ritualists tend not to think of themselves as actors;
they are not performing, they are doing. There is no doubt that a performance
can be powerful and is capable of producing a mixture of feelings to include
catharsis. So, too, can ritual.

The *Liji* or *Book of Rites* of Confucianism teaches that ritual can organize
individuals into cohesive groups. This grand unity or grand way eliminates
self-centeredness and discord. Ritual is "the tie that binds." In the western
world, the Enlightenment taught autonomy and rationalism. Ritual came

under suspicion and was often discredited. It was deemed ineffective and, even, detrimental to the human psyche. But this "advancement" in the western world was, in fact, not a step forward but a step backward. Social fragmentation spread resulting in a lack of social bonding, poor communication, and, at the extreme, conflict. Huxley also suggested that, since ritualization is a socialization function, the lack of it, the trend to become devoid of ritual, is "playing with fire." So, too, suggested Joseph Campbell as noted above.

A great ill of the modern era is the impoverishment of ritual. Rites of passage such as weddings and funerals have become trivialized and minimalized. Everything is now prepackaged and plastic wrapped. What passes for ritual is a drive-through window in Las Vegas. There is a longing for ritual in the modern world. But care must be taken not to invent or borrow actions from other cultures to fulfil the need. The dynamic loss of public ritual in Europe contributed to the rise of Nazism in Germany replete with its borrowing of myriad rituals and processions. How, though, does an organization teach useful ritual that will properly instruct initiates and protect the culture from further erosion?

NOTES

1. Guy Davenport. *The Geography of the Imagination* (San Francisco: North Point Press, 1981), 134.
2. http://www.springfieldspringfield.co.uk/movie_script.php?movie=brideshead-revisited.
3. Catherine Bell. *Ritual: Perspectives and Dimensions.* (New York: Oxford University Press, (2007), 223.
4. Elias Ashmole. *Memoirs of the Life of that Learned Antiquary, Elias Ashmole, Esq.* Farmington, Mich.: Gale ECCO Press, 2010, 26.
5. "Baltimore Convention, 1843" located at http://www.themasonictrowel.com/masonic_talk/stb/stbs/36-01.htm
6. Peter McLaren, "Rethinking Ritual," in *ETC: A Review of General Semantics, Vol. 41, No. 3* (Fall 1984), 272.
7. Walter L. Brenneman et. Al., *The Seeing Eye: Hermeneutical Phenomenology in the Study of Religion* (Pennsylvania: The Pennsylvania State University Press, 1982), 112.
8. Barry Stephenson, *Ritual: A Very Short Introduction* (New York: Oxford University Press, 2015), 22.
9. Douglas A. Marshall, "Behavior, Belonging, and Belief: A Theory of Ritual Practice" in *Social Theory, Vol. 20 No. 39 (November 2002)*, 374.
10. Marshall, "Behavior, Belonging." 9.
11. Joseph Campbell, *The Power of Myth.* (New York: Anchor Books,1991), p. 38.
12. Steven Lukes. *Emile Durkheim: His Life and Work: A Historical and Critical Study* (New York: Penguin, 1977), 471.
13. Henri Hurbert & Marcel Mauss, *Sacrifice: Its Nature and Functions* [1898], trans. W.D. Hall (Chicago: University of Chicago, 1964), 8-9.
14. Robert Segal. "The Myth-Ritualist Theory of Religion" in *Journal for the Scientific Study of Religion 19, No. 2, 1980,* 173-185.
15. Julian. Huxley. "A Discussion on Ritualization of Behavior in Animals and Man" in Philosophical *Transactions of the Royal Society,* series B, 251, 1966, 247-525.
16. Richard Schechner. *Between Theatre and Anthropology.* (Philadelphia: University of Pennsylvania Press, 1985), 52.

Chapter Two

More Ritual Light

The mysteries were instituted in order to protect the marvels of the common-place from those who would devalue them.

Figure 2.1. Ritual 2.

Far too many well-educated people incorrectly consider ritual as incredibly difficult. It isn't. It can be taught and it is best taught to and in groups at a level and with an intensity of mind-body interdependence unusual to most educational settings. You cannot teach ritual sitting at a desk or watching a TV screen. Nor can it be taught from books. Ritual is exclusively oral and physical thus requiring direct human participation and interaction.

Ritual is all about the five senses. It is a means for articulating ideas that enable us to connect content and action as it deepens understanding. It is human communication in its highest form with that communication being defined as symbolic interaction. Suzanne Langer notes that a symbol enables people to think about, understand, and react to something apart from its immediate presence. A symbol is "an instrumental thought." [1] We apportion to symbols meanings which result in emotional responses. But the meaning assigned to a symbol and our emotional response can undergo radical change or, even, drastic reversal. Consider the swastika appropriated by the Nazi party and the palm up, arm extended salute used during the pledge of allegiance to the U.S. flag prior to World War II. Both symbols underwent dramatic change and were quickly discarded.

The meaning of a symbol is based upon an agreement within the group. In order for language (the method for communicating meaning) to function successfully, shared meaning is required. We must agree that what we are talking about is "what we are talking about." When we use a word, the listener creates a mental image of the object and while that mental image may vary in details, it is the basic concept that counts. It is critical to communication that we agree upon the proposition—cow, a domestic animal with four legs, a tail, a head, that goes "moo" and produces milk that humans can drink —not necessarily the details of color, breed, or weight.

A great deal of human behavior involves communication and meets symbolic needs thus becoming symbolic acts (speech for verbal symbolization and action for nonverbal symbolization) which leads to ritual. George Herbert Mead's definitive work *Mind, Self and Society* provides the foundation for understanding symbolic interaction. In order for humans to cooperate, they must first come to an agreed upon understanding of each other's intentions. Symbol-using interaction serves that function. Humans, through their mental processing, plan and rehearse their symbolic behavior so as to better prepare themselves for social interaction. And while Kenneth Burke is recognized for his explanation of the use of dramatic metaphor in communication[2] , he also discussed how individuals use ritual to present themselves to others. Finally, Hugh Duncan stresses the importance of the symbol in transmitting meaning.[3] People assume roles, he suggests, stressing that "Social order is created and sustained in social dramas through intensive and frequent communal presentations."[4]

Symbols function also to synthesize the tone, character, and quality of human life giving it a moral and aesthetic style and mood. They provide a picture of how things should be. They represent sets of acts; establish powerful and long-lasting moods and motivations; formulate conceptions in general; clothe perceptions with an aura of factuality; and "establish moods and motivations that seem uniquely realistic."[5]

Symbols are vehicles for the conception of meaning and are abstractions fixed in perceptible form with concrete embodiments of ideas, attitudes, judgements, longings, and beliefs. They are the key to understanding. A blue print for a building is a symbol. It is not the actual building, just an agreed upon plan that contains symbols that have meaning to those involved in its construction. In man, his DNA does not predict his ability to engage in the building trade. That ability requires planning, education, training, supervision, and repetition as well as a concept of what is to be built presented in symbolic form. Symbols are blueprints or textbooks not buildings. And DNA is a beginning, a plan, not an outcome. The proper manipulation of significant symbols gives them graphic power and enables man to attain his destiny—the end product.

In Freemasonry, symbols are intertransportable. They mean different things at different times and on different levels. They shape our ritual into a distinctive set of tendencies, capacities, propensities, skills, habits, liabilities, and pronenesses as they give character to the flow of our activity and the quality of our experience. The legend and the meanings of the symbols are learned by heart, but the moods the symbols in the legend induce range from melancholy to joy; from confidence to pity; from exalted to bland. Communication, then, is a complex process that utilizes symbols to transmit meaning as well as emotion and to socialize the individual. A primary form of this transmission and socialization is ritual.

The meaning of a symbol is often elusive, but that meaning is capable of being discovered and understood through investigation and explanation, and it is then possible to convey that meaning to others. And just as language is constituted of units—sounds and words—so too is ritual constituted of separate symbolic acts. But the meaning of both the symbols and the ritual are grasped fully only through cultural transformation or initiation.

Humans are cultural animals and prefer to live in societies. People are, Aquinas wrote in *City of God* "bound together by a common agreement as to the objects of their love."[6] The flaw in human reasoning, though, is that while the lowest levels of life described in Maslow's "Hierarchy of Needs" as physiological and safety (air, water, food, personal security, and health) are self-evident, higher requirements such as love, esteem, and self-actualization, because they are elevated and internal, are less clear and less understood. At these upper levels there is a weakened sense of certainty and stability. In the twenty-first century, communities or societies with common interests serve to ameliorate that concern by bringing members into harmony through philosophic interchange addressing questions about higher certainties. And while authority is often rooted in tradition and custom, when reason is added to the mix, traditions and customs may provide guidance for human thought and action.

In *Laws*, considered Plato's most political writing, he tells the parable of the Athenian stranger who said "let our race be something that is not lowly, then, if that is what you cherish, but worthy of a certain seriousness."[7] The Platonic metaphor suggests that many of us can only "stare reality in the face [and] the truth is too strong for most eyes."[8] A natural response to this has been through the use of esotericism and ritual as discussed in Chapter VI. Ritual, therefore, is that which is natural in form and content even if it appears to be highly elaborate and filled with symbolism and allegory. Ritual, though, tends to be celebratory in nature and is experienced at various levels through different senses. It can be a therapeutic and cathartic tool but it can also be a formula that enables us to interpret our drives and motivations in terms of brotherly love and respect for tradition and others. Ritual is not necessarily to be understood, however, but to be felt and experienced. It is a celebration of life and its experiences as well as of human striving and motivation. It may well be a higher route to a fuller understanding of the human and the divine.

The Latin word which provides the root for the modern word "ritual" referred specifically to the Roman judicial concept of the correct way to perform which had been proven true through experience and expressed as an action. It was those actions which were considered normal, natural, and true. Ritual functions by enabling the human brain to focus on the question or object at hand in such a manner as to direct the individual and the group to a shared meaning that serves the best interest of those involved.

Our ancient brethren labored diligently over centuries to develop and understand their Craft; to perpetuate its history, knowledge, and identity through symbols and allegory; and to provide proper initiatic experiences for novices by introducing them to the Fraternity through a system of ever higher levels of knowledge (degrees) imparted through ritual. Knoop and Jones note that by the early years of the eighteenth century, Freemasons had expanded their practices (ritual) by assigning to their working tools special moral and spiritual meaning, and by utilizing those symbols in their ritual. These early speculative Brethren conceived of something apart from the immediate or practical nature of the object. The symbols became "instruments of thought" that required further study and contemplation to reach a full understanding of their meaning.

Ritual utilizes shared meanings to transmit to all involved as well as through generations the principles, tenets, and beliefs of the institution. It comes to us in six forms: formalism, traditionalism, invariance, sacred, and performance. It is further subcategorized by genre to include rites of passage, commemorative rites, rites of communion, rites of affliction, and rites of festival. Paramount for humans is the fact that ritual enhances meaning and understanding as it furthers learning. We memorize the catechisms and degree work--learn the basic principles—and then we progress to the application of that information in our search for and attainment of higher, more significant knowledge—more and further light.

In Freemasonry, our forms and ceremonies--our rituals--perform not only as formal, traditional exercises that create an *esprit de corps* as well as a shared experience and language, they also provide the means for the transmission of our traditions and to establish for the Brethren the higher meaning of the signs, symbols, allegories, and landmarks of our Craft as well enabling them to fully comprehend those special meanings. And while the practical aspect of Masonic ritual is important—opening and closing of the Lodge, the conferral of Degrees, the installation of officers, the internment of the dead and should be uniform utilizing an agreed-upon language, symbolization and action--it is the meaning that is paramount, not the specific action or performance.

Through ritual, those involved are able to interact with the world that surrounds them in a manner agreed upon by all through tradition and repetition. It simplifies the uncertainty of events and communications by imposing a coherent system that facilitates cataloging, categorizing, and understanding. Doing makes believing and understanding easier.

Predictability is essential to human functioning yet we live in a very unpredictable world. When you pick up the phone you fully expect to hear a dial tone and when you dial a number you fully and properly expect to be connected with the intended party. When this does not happen you grow frustrated and react accordingly. The same happens when you work at a computer. You press the keys anticipating a specific response. Frustration again arises when that does not happen—as so many customer service representatives can testify. The same process applies in human communication. When we give a specific verbal cue to another person, we anticipate that we will receive an appropriate anticipated response. When that does not happen, our expectations are defeated and, again, we become frustrated. Ritual is no different. It is, by its very nature, predictable, and when that prediction is not fulfilled, disappointment, even frustration is the end product.

Human life is defined by a series of choices in an unpredictable world, and the more choices we confront, the easier it is for us to become stressed. Ritual fulfills a necessary psychological function for humans as they go through their daily lives by addressing directly such issues of choice. As Clark Gable points out in "It Happened One Night," even how you dress or undress is ritualized. Ritual, unlike daily life, is predictable and that predictability generates a calming effect in the human psyche. It serves that same psychic function by facilitating the individual's accurate prediction of what will happen next and, when it does happen, it further empowers the psyche by generating ego fulfillment and self enhancement from having made an accurate prediction.

A majority of human fears can be dealt with through ritual. Young children engage in ritualistic behaviors such as saying certain words, prayers, or stories at bedtime; performing special bedtime actions; or requiring the presence of a special and specific symbol—a teddy bear, for example. This fulfills a child's need for routine and structure. Such constructive human ritual gives order to daily routine and provides for "peace of mind' in both children and adults. But there is a difference between healthy positive rituals and those that are destructive or addictive. Healthy rituals or routines may and often are altered, interrupted, resumed, and, even discarded as time and circumstance may dictate. The teddy bear finds its way from the child's cuddle, to the shelf, and then to the closet or trunk. This may be done without the loss of the ritual's impact or a reduction in the pleasure received when engaged in ritual actions because we tend to replace one ritual with another which we deem more mature or more reflective of our current status in life. Unhealthy rituals, however, being addictive in nature, cannot be easily discarded, amended, or broken without marked psychological damage.

Normal routines and rituals have a calming effect on humans by reducing fear. For example, most humans fear loss—of parents, objects, and friends. We overcome this fear through the ritual of collecting be it photographs, rocks, dolls, coins, or baseball cards. A healthy ritual (or hobby) does not interfere with one's ability to function or take up too much time or space. It is a normal human activity utilized to deal with the uncertainty of existence.

Ritual facilitates learning by enabling the ritualists to connect the inner emotional experience to that of the audience through systematized words, gestures, and movements. This is the product of a thorough understanding of how humans behave when responding to various emotional and real life situations, and by transferring these observations to the ritual's structure. Ritualistic gestures, movements, and words must not, however, be stereotyped or melodramatic; rather they should be performed in a natural manner which results in a relatively predictable emotional connectivity between the presenter and the audience.

Ritual also serves the interest of the ritualists or actor/performer. Humans by their very nature respond more to actions than they do to words— "Do as I do" versus "Do as I say." Telling a child or an adult to do as you say, not as you do, seldom produces the desired behavior and often results in derision as well as a "failure to communicate." Behavior, and all ritual is behavior, is a much stronger motivational force than is simple verbal communication. And when actions are coupled with clear, distinct, descriptive words, the learning experience works even faster and with significantly better comprehension and retention.

Ritual functions also to facilitate and enhance learning through observation and imitation. Experience is definitely a great and wonderful teacher, but you cannot experience everything yourself. You can, however, observe the actions of others engaged in a ritualistic experience and through that observation learn and imitate.

Psychologists generally refer to ritual as a form of repetitive behavior engaged in by persons to neutralize or prevent anxiety and to help human's address that which is new, strange, and different. This definition is important to Freemasonry because our ritual and its content is not only central to understanding the Craft's allegories but also to neutralizing the anxiety initiates and ritualists often feel prior to and during the ceremony. Ritual is both a form of internal communication and a means for facilitating external communication as well as inner reflection. Ritual is intended to be performed as well as contemplated. To perform any ritual at its most impressive and instructional, especially one of a Masonic nature, we must reach an agreed upon understanding of the symbolization involved and be able to interpret it properly to the candidate by utilizing our physical and oral skills. The performance and content of the ritual may vary, as it does between Masonic Jurisdictions and, even, Lodges, but that should not reduce its impact or intensity. The ritualistic experience, the centrality of ritual to our Craft, or the ability of those rituals and symbols to link us together through a common belief system and a shared communication experience remain unchanged from generation to generation.

Humans engage in spiritual ceremonies or rituals because they provide comfort; are engaging; possess intrinsic power; are familiar; teach; because they illustrate; because they reduce anxiety; because they enhance performance; require personal participation; make us part of a community; provide physical and psychological benefits; and because they have a direct influence upon what comes after as well as our interpretation of what came before. Ritual provides us with a safe place, free from the worries of daily life. It is an anchor line that links us to a solid foundation as it enables us to mend a broken down emotional system.

Ritual gives shape, order, and identity to daily life. A great deal of religious ritual is oriented to the calendar enabling us to celebrate and acknowledge the passage of time. Other religious rituals, communion, for example, link us to our past and, since done with other people, make us part of a larger community. The power of ritual is linked to the number of participants and, as with a wedding or funeral, celebrates life events common to all humanity. But ritual is not meaningless repetition. Each time a ritual is performed, we discover something new. Ritual is, to draw from Aristotle again, cathartic: it provides us with an emotional release (sometimes strong). It is not "mumbo-jumbo:" the words and actions have meaning both intrinsically and extrinsically. Ritual is physiologically and psychologically appealing because it enables us to utilize space and time to express ourselves and demonstrate our involvement in the process. It can, however, lose its power if too protracted or too esoteric.

Ritual is not easy to perform or appreciate. Dedication, thoughtfulness, and concentration on the part of both participant and spectator are required. When engaged in ritual, we are capable of shutting out the intrusions of daily life and focus on internal reflection. Ritual, when properly performed, makes us fully aware of the moment and cognizant of the situation. A perfectly performed ritual is similar, in emotional response, to a perfectly performed symphony. The sour note, the misplaced beat, the break in rhythm diffuses or, even, eliminates enjoyment and psychological fulfillment. The perfectly performed composition moves us to exceed the commonplace and respond on a higher plane. Ritual works in an identical manner: the closer to perfection, the greater the impact of the ceremony.

Ritual is most comfortable when we have mastered it. The mastery of ritual is directly related to our personal concept of accomplishment and well-being. We strive for perfection, though we settle for excellence or less. We are not perfect creatures, but when we perform ritual in a proper manner and are fully confident in our performance, our level of comfort increases. This level of comfort is transmitted to other participants as well as to spectators and becomes an expression of the power of the performance. When great actors appear on stage, their confidence in their performance contributes to the willing suspension of disbelief and enables the audience to participate in the dramatic event to the fullest extent. So it is with ritual, the more confident the ritualist, the more compelling the ritual. It is comfortable because it is familiar. It is predictable in a chaotic, unpredictable world. When an individual departs for work in the morning there is an unpredictable aspect to both the journey and all possible future events which may be discomforting. With ritual, we know what is coming. It isn't a surprise. It doesn't change and, while change may be the one constant in life, it is disconcerting. Through ritual we neutralize anxiety. Well-rehearsed and performed ritual accomplishes it transformative task by utilizing a combination of physiological and psychological inputs to establish well-being.

Ritual requires us to participate either directly as an actor or indirectly as an observer. In both roles we are engaged in the event. As in sports, both the player and the spectator participate in the game and, in turn, in the win or loss. For both the participant and the observer of ritual, there is a type of mystical inspiration. It is a shared experience, but the level of involvement determines the degree to which the observer partakes of the experience. There are myriad reasons for engaging in ritual to include eustress (positive stress), escape, entertainment, group affiliation, self-esteem, and, even, peer pressure and as well as family needs. But it serves a specific purpose both in culture and in Freemasonry. In Freemasonry it is used to teach the signs, symbols, allegories, tokens, and the meaning of the Craft through the various degrees. Lodge ritual also serves to unify the fraternal community and to provide an agreed upon purpose and direction to all activity. And it enhances learning because it is composed of physical acts coupled with verbal expressions. Learning utilizing a single sense such as hearing is possible, but it is enriched when pictures and action are added to the words.

Ritual is an organized communication performance that expresses a shared experience and, is most effective, when repeated on a regular basis to insure familiarity with its aspects and a level of perfection in its performance. Ritual is important because it provides for a renewal of our shared or common experiences and gives legitimacy to what we are doing. In a very real way, ritual makes us free men while enabling us to interact with others. Masonic ritual involves the ritualists, the spectator, and the initiate to create a total experience. It impacts on consciousness and changes the body by requiring it to meet ritualistic needs. It is an experience which remains with the candidate forever. In Freemasonry it is intended to be an intense process during which the neophyte undergoes a reinvention of self.

Freemasonry utilizes symbols to express, through its ritual, a communal experience and this same ritual helps us remember, renew, and refresh our links to our past, our community, and our inner selves. The repetition inherent in ritual is markedly similar to the social rituals that enable us to engage with family, friends, community, and strangers. At the same time, ritual is storytelling at its sincerest and complete. The three degrees of Freemasonry tell a complete story—the allegory of the building of King Solomon's Temple and Hiram Abiff. They form a "rite" in that they refer to a series of events and are governed by proscribed actions. In the first degree the candidate enters a symbolic temple and is introduced to the architecture, ornaments, and furnishing of a Lodge. In the second degree, representing a passage from childhood to the middle years, he is instructed in architecture and the liberal arts. In the third degree he learns of the Hiramic Legend and that once a Master Mason, he has access to the *sanctum sanctorum* as well as the knowledge vested there.

Masonic ritual and its utilization of symbolic communication leads all Brothers to a fuller understanding of the Craft as a representation of the human psyche. It was, by the eighteenth century, an approach to the essence of the Renaissance and the Enlightenment expressed as a mystery. Divided now into three levels, it represents the physical world, the quest for knowledge and enlightenment, and, finally, the melding of body with spirit. The rituals performed refresh for the Brethren the meaning of power and personal strength as they orient the newcomer to our organization while reaffirming for all involved the meaning of their quest. Further, our ritual introduces and refreshes our sense of group identity as it teaches us the courtesies and obligations of our Craft. It also teaches us the culture of the organization by enabling us to "learn the ropes" through a series of performances. Although this may be accomplished by direct instruction, engagement in ritual enables us to interpret the events in terms of the organizational perspective—to be part of the group—through physical action. Ritual, therefore, contributes directly to understanding the cultural meaning of Freemasonry.

Joseph Campbell writes that ritual is meant to convey an inner reality, though now, for too many, it has become merely form without substance; action without meaning. Society without ritual, he suggests, lacks the method to introduce the young into the tribe. Children, in order to function rationally in society, need to be twice born, he notes. Masonic ritual serves that exact function. Ritual or degree work in the Lodge is the essential element of Freemasonry. It transforms a man into a Brother, a Freemason. It is designed to impact directly on the inner life of the candidates and Brothers, and should never be thought of as empty, meaningless ceremony. It must be respected and performed with reverence if it is to be effective, impressive, and if it is to continue into time immemorial.

Thus there is no place for mirth or frivolity or laughter or whispering in our ritual. The focal point of all of our work is *The Holy Bible* and, as such, it deserves our respect as it serves to temper our actions. Our ritual is not worthy of applause because it transcends all that is praiseworthy. The candidate has come to us of his own free will and we welcome him into our fellowship as expressively and spiritually as possible. He should be the center of attention, not the ritualists. To engage in applause or side-line comments during ritual or exemplification destroys the illusion and significantly reduces the impact of the event on all involved, especially those at its focus—the candidates or Brothers. Our degrees are an allegory of good and evil, of life itself. Death is prominent throughout the Third Degree and specifically referenced in the First Degree. Our ritual is intended to speak directly to the inner life of the candidate. To do this the candidate must not only hear and perform, he must witness the intensity of the moment as expressed through proper decorum and dress.

Decorum refers to the proper or appropriate style for a presentation or ritual. It is not only the proper or right social behavior fitting to the situation; it is also an elevated standard of behavior as well and a strong adherence to proper procedure. It includes appropriate, often symbolic, behavior as well as an elevated level of dignity in speech, dress, and action. In Freemasonry, proper decorum is not something to be determined by the individual Brother according to his own tastes. It manifests itself through its demonstration of respect for the Craft and the Brethren. "Sunday best" implied not only an expression of esteem for the church, religion in general, and God; it also implied a respect for self. It demonstrated a congregant's beliefs about the importance of the Deity and served as a fulfillment of a religious obligation to give unto God only the best. Freemasonry is not nor has it ever been a religion, but it does espouse a similar moral light and is thus worthy of a similar demonstration of respect. *The Regius Manuscript* or poem, which dates from the late fourteenth century, as well as succeeding constitutions and charges, required those who were "made a Mason" to pay due respect to the Craft through their proper behavior and appropriate attire.

There is no doubt that how a person dresses is a significant factor in the establishment of first impressions. Based on the photographic record present in most modern Lodges, Brethren in the nineteenth and first half of the twentieth centuries exercised a high standard of dress in the Lodge—Sunday best, if you will. During Masonic ritual, especially degree work, elevated levels of dress and decorum enhance the overall experience to the betterment of all involved. The general rule, outside the United States, is that a dark suit and appropriate tie are required to attend Lodge with Masters often dressed in cutaways and top hat and other officers in proper evening dress such as a tux. The question a Freemason should ask himself is this: "In terms of showing reverence and respect for the Craft, is that my best, and is that what my best should be?"[9]

Appropriate dress "sets the stage" and strengthens the ritualistic experience as it solemnizes and honors the experience. Actors require costumes to "set the mood" and "establish character." So, too, does Masonic ritual. Consider a priest at Mass: would the service have the same impact if he wasn't wearing liturgical vestments? Military chaplains, even in combat zones, strive to maintain some level of appropriate, liturgical dress to formalize and solemnize the ritual. Catholic and Episcopal chaplains in chasuble and stole standing on muddy firebases in Vietnam bringing comfort to soldiers was a common sight for 10 years. Their stoles, muddy and blood-stained, were prominently visible when giving Last Rites during a firefight. Part of the comfort they offered came from the soldiers recognizing them by the clothes (vestments) they wore. Those vestments were what set them outside the profane and the reality of the moment. Appropriate attire, especially for degree teams, can accomplish the same.

Good ritual like good music is a function of pacing and rhythm. Rhythm enhances emotional responses as is suggested in the lecture for the Fellow Craft Degree during the explanation of the art of music. It impacts directly upon human psychology and physiology through a pattern of regular or irregular beats which make for either a strong or weak response. It can make the heart beat faster and the muscles tense because it is the pattern of the flow of both sound and action in parallel with human internal rhythms. The proper use of rhythm not only serves to enhance the ritualistic experience; it also enables the human brain to more fully comprehend the situation through a pattern of regular stresses which facilitate memorization. Rhythm in ritual identifies that which is important.

Ritual is, by its nature, repetitive. Repetition is the most intuitive learning technique and is documented in both Chinese and Egyptian records dating to 3,000 B.C.E. or before. It requires us to do the same thing several times in the same way. In teaching, an ancient maxim is to say and/or do the same thing three times and so it is with our ritual. This repetition not only provides for better retention but it also marks those parts of our work which are to be remembered. Repetition enables us to efficiently store information and guides to action in our memory. It strengthens skill at both the conscious and subconscious level. And when a skill has been set through repetition—riding a bike—it is possible to quickly recover that skill at a later date.

Virtually all rote learning is in based memorization and repetition. And while repetition alone does not lead directly to understanding, it is the first step. Memorization facilitates human experience by reducing the necessity to think about and analyze each individual step or function thus facilitating analysis and learning at a higher level. "Practice makes perfect" goes the old saying. Masonic ritual requires practice, probably not as intense or extensive as that engaged in by a professional actor or athlete, but never-the-less it is essential to the ritualistic experience.

In order to engage in ritual, both the ritualists and candidate must focus on the task at hand. For the candidate this is easy. In the typical Masonic ritual, he is blindfolded and therefore cannot see. For the ritualists who can see this is more difficult and requires practice and clarity of mind. Great actors have confidence in their ability and their knowledge of their part, but they also report that they "don't see the audience" or hear them. The part has consumed them as has the moment and all external distractions are eliminated through concentration. "Talk to the first row in the balcony" is a common expression indicating not only the need to project one's voice, but also the need not to see the audience individually, if at all. Masonic ritualists should heed this advice by focusing on the candidate and the internal experience thus shutting out external events.

Much has been said and written over the years about the nature of Masonic ritual with some suggesting that it should be stripped, condensed, or even abandoned. The significant loss of membership in the Independent Order of Odd Fellows as discussed by Ted Hendon in his article "Of Freemasons, Odd Fellows, and Passenger Pigeons" and discussed elsewhere in this text may serve as an example of a path not to be considered. In 1922 there were more than 2.7 million Odd Fellows. By 1979, that number had dropped to about 243,000—a reduction in membership of more than ninety percent. And while this organization now reports more than 600,000 members including women, that is still only about twenty-two percent of its former numbers.

The marked decline in the Odd Fellow fraternity is generally attributed to several factors. First, the organization kept its fees and dues at an extremely low level. Secondly, even though the fraternity included degree work, catechisms, and ritual, their use was often not enforced and too often neglected based on the incorrect assumption that "modern young men" were unwilling to commit the time and effort necessary to mastering the traditional foundation blocks of the fraternity. Thirdly, there was, within the order, a move away from the requirement that a member be selected by a unanimous secret ballot. And finally, the order focused more on external social work and charity than on internal education and moral instruction. The creation of the New Deal in the 1930s and the multitude of governmental social programs that followed, significantly eroded the Odd Fellows reason for being. Their lodges lost their ability to confer degrees or even generate members proficient in their ritual. The Odd Fellows did, however, make a positive step in 1971 when they removed from their governing documents the requirement that member be of the "white" race only. None of this, though, resulted in the return of the Odd Fellows to its former status.

The argument is often made that this is a new age worthy of new traditions; that old traditions are mere baggage keeping away members "in droves;" and that memorization along with ritualization demands too much time and effort to be attractive to media savvy young men. Along with this plethora of reasons has come numerous suggestions, all well intended, and some jurisdictions have followed them. This loss of tradition and reduction in spiritual enrichment through ritual is not compatible, however, with what young men express when asked about their expectations and the attraction of Freemasonry as noted in the Pew and the Social Institute Research Institute's surveys. Both point to a need for traditional spiritual expression through ritual; rigorous leadership selection and training; enhanced mentoring; and an adherence to traditional values as expressed in our ritual. A parable is now in order to express esoterically the issue of understanding the place of tradition in our ritual. Below is Maimonides' parable of a great ruler and his edifice which speaks to the pitfalls of not understanding or trusting those who came before and who erected this mighty ritual structure.

I TELL YOU A PARABLE

A wise ruler of a very large empire erected a magnificent palace of immeasurable dimensions and extraordinary architecture. He gathered around him assistants qualified to produce the work and provided them with the high-quality instruments to pursue their labors. This magnificent structure, though not of ordinary construction, was pleasing to the eye and served its purpose. It was durable and functional—it inculcated the mysteries of the kingdom to its subjects. From outside it was perplexing, but from within it was full of light, knowledge, and coherence.

There were those in the country, especially wise men skilled in architecture, who were offended by its very structure. It had few windows and it wasn't easy to gain entrance. The doors did not seem well placed and the gates were guarded. These learned men could not grasp that each apartment received its light, as did the whole, not from without but from within and above. They could not comprehend that those who entered went of their own free will and that the entrance provided them with the surest route to their objective.

Accordingly, these wise men explained the words, symbols, and architecture as they saw them according to their preconceived ideas of the plan. They paid no heed to those who worked within the palace and had neither the time nor the inclination to discuss with them its architecture, even denouncing those who supported the edifice's design as despoilers of the palace itself.

One terrible night, the watchman called "Fire! Fire!" and everyone leapt from their beds scurrying through the darkness squabbling with each other about how best to save the edifice. Each said that they had the proper plan to save the palace based on their experience and expertise. But none sought to find a bucket of water to throw on the reported flames. If there had, in fact, been a fire, the palace would have lain in ruins at dawn, but the watchman was wrong. He had mistaken the northern lights for a conflagration and the glowing interior light confused the experts. What each quibbler failed to acknowledge or accept was that the great and wise ruler had built his magnificent palace on a sound foundation based on ancient plans give him by his ancestors and that it was infused with interior not exterior light.

Freemasonry must not lose the light given by its wise founders over four hundred years ago (extant minutes from Edinburgh Lodge No. 1 date to 1599). It must continue to strive to promote brotherly love and affection, and to exemplify these attributes through its ritual. Freemasonry provides light through ritual which represents the letter as well as the spirit of the Craft's ancient beliefs. It ceaselessly strives to promote human brotherhood and is inevitably put at risk when social, political, or religious divisions are permitted to intrude. Freemasonry is not dogmatic and through figurative language endeavors to illustrate and amplify that which is self-evident. Freemasonry has its riddles and paradoxes. It often seems to use ellipsis and aposiopesis to deny the casual viewer a definitive statement or definition, but our ritual fills these ellipsis and aposiopesis not with words but through action with meaning.

The Lodge is to Freemasonry what the church edifice is to religion. No conclusions should be drawn from the external prosperity or inner trappings of a building about the faith of its members. The two do not always go together. It is the internal, not the external which has enabled Freemasonry to survive and even prosper for more than four centuries. Ritual is the single most important aspect of our observance of the Craft. Human history has been enriched through the extensive use of ritual by all societies. Ritual appeals to us because it provides us with a window into our shared culture. It is central to both religious and secular society because it generates an emotional response and because it is understandable. It is a physical manifestation of an internal, emotional experience.

Ritual appeals to us because it is experiential and analytical. It engulfs the total person, transporting him into another mode of existence. It has persuasive, even mystical power, and is filled with extraordinary personalities. It enables us to do what we are thinking about, and at the same time, reflect more fully upon the experience. Masonic ritual enables us to understand our symbols and history, and while it may be "scary" to some and misunderstood by others, proper performance and appreciation of our ritual serves to facilitate full development of the Symbolic Lodge and the Brotherhood. It was our ritual that attracted great and learned men to Freemasonry in the seventeenth, eighteenth, nineteenth, and twentieth centuries, and it serves the same purpose today.

Ultimately, man can adapt himself to anything, but he cannot deal with chaos. Ritual is not chaos. Therefore, one of the most important assets of Freemasonry is that symbolic ritual which orients our lives and our relationships through what we do. Ritual enables us to explain and demonstrate things which cry out for explanation. It is the foundation not only of our Craft but of our very existence.

NOTES

1. Susanne Langer, *Philosophy in a New Key* (Cambridge, MA: Harvard University Press, 1942), 26.

2. Stephen Littlejohn, *Theories of Human Communication* (Columbus, OH: Charles E. Merrill Publishing Company, 1978), 68-72.

3. Hugh Duncan, *Symbols in Society* (New York: Oxford University Press, 1968), 60.

4. Duncan, *Symbols in Society,* 60.

5. Clifford Geertz, *The Interpretation of Cultures: Selected Essays by Clifford Geert* New York: Basic Books 1973), 90.

6. R.W. Dyson (ed.), *Augustine: The City of God against the Pagans.* (Cambridge UK: Cambridge University Press, 1998), 960.

7. Plato, *The Laws of Plato,* Thomas Pangle (trans.). (Chicago: The University of Chicago Press, 1980), 194.

8. Arthur M. Melzer, *Philosophy Between the Lines.* (Chicago: University of Chicago Press, 2014), 190.

9. Andrew Hammer. *Observing the Craft: The Pursuit of Excellence in Masonic Labor and Observance.* (San Francisco, CA: Mindhive Books, 2012), 85.

Chapter Three

Further Ritual Light

The sauce to meat is ceremony; Meetings were bare without it.
—*Macbeth* by Shakespeare

Figure 3.1. Ritual 3.

Clear definitions are essential to the understanding of ritual. *Ritual*, therefore, is defined as special action and *myth* as stories that often explain origins. Myths come in narrative form and may be acted as well as recited or read. *Symbols* are things to which we assign meaning. Symbols often serve to maintain the status quo just as much as they serve to mark life-changing events or episodes. The basic requirements for ritual are symbols, narrative, and, to some extent, culture. The concept of "culture" arose in the nineteenth century as a means for the discussion of how humans behave, especially in groups. Culture transcends nature, environment, and heredity, thus encompassing everything associated with mankind. It is not only what humans carry with them; it is what is passed on through means other than biological. Culture is learned, not genetically programmed. It comes with a set of rules, procedures, and assumptions with some, but by no means all, being moralistic. Culture is not consciously taught but rather acquired in the community. It is ubiquitous but not universally the same.

And just as humans use language to transmit their culture, so too do they use symbolism metaphor, and ritual. The human mind functions symbolically, wrote Alfred North Whitehead, and Clifford Geertz speaks of symbols as "vehicles for conception." In fact, all human language is symbolic as are a vast majority of human actions. Symbols express both importance and emotional attachment with Edward Sapir noting that the significance of the symbol is often out of proportion to its mere form which may be quite trivial. Symbols are complex, multilayered expressions with emotional and cognitive value. Symbols do not provide a clear definition; they merely point us in a certain direction.

Metaphors, on the other hand, are figures of speech that use symbolism. They compare two things that are dissimilar and indicate that they do have something in common. A metaphor assigns a different meaning to a word thus making it symbolic. A metaphor is one type of trope which is a figure of speech which symbolically links two things. What most people refer to as metaphor, is, in fact, a trope. A trope, in turn, is distinguished from a simile in that a simile makes an overt comparison and often uses the word "like." Going a step further we find a metonym which links two things that may be somehow connected: umbrella and rain; Neville Chamberlain and appeasement; cowboys and saddles; Dodge City and gunfights. Most metonyms demonstrate a physical connection or a logical contiguity. Thus a Mason may be linked with a square, level, compasses, or apron.

Metaphors or tropes are often used to both teach and persuade through rhetoric. They are a staple of oratory and there is nothing inherently wrong with persuading using language laced with metaphors. In fact, cultural persuasion and instruction are often a matter of selecting the right metaphor to transmit the meaning. The key to interpreting the metaphor is to reach an understanding of the attributes the metaphor attempts to express. Paying attention and respecting local knowledge or group knowledge is essential. The British, for example, paid no attention to Inuit traditions of using dogs, sleds, and kayaks instead relying upon ponies while attempting to reach the polar regions resulting in men hauling their sledges over the ice and losing the race. The problem with modern man is that he has become too detached from the natural world. He fails to grasp the relevant allusions found in all classical literature, especially *The Bible*—and in Freemasonry.

Hiram Abiff, the chief architect at the building of King Solomon's Temple, is murdered shortly before its completion. Fifteen fellow craft plot the assassination but, after further reflection on the proposed act, twelve of them recant and confess the conspiracy. The narrative is that of conspiracy, intrigue, murder, retribution, reconsideration, confession, and, in a way, liberation from illusion and ignorance. It is not a narrative of resurrection as so many anti-Masonic groups and writers suggest. At best, it is a reflection on renewal or more properly a never-ending quest for that renewal, but it also encompasses the process of returning something to its original state or returning something that was stolen or misplaced. No one returns from the grave in the allegory nor is anything fully restored. What was lost remains lost and is replaced with a substitute. The message is found in the pointed images in the ritual that encompass the triumph of good over evil, personal integrity, and the ability of man to address his shortcomings (sins) and to seek redemption. Why, though, did the creators of this saga elect to use fifteen and why did twelve confess but only three complete the quest? Why choose these numbers? Why not eight, ten, or twenty? An analysis of classical literature and attention to local knowledge as well as group traditions may provide answers.

The simple answer is that numbers are symbolic as well as real. Some Masonic scholars suggest that the number three is used repeatedly in a symbolic manner because it fits so neatly into the three-degree structure: symbolic Lodges have three degrees; there are three principle officers; and the Fraternity has three principle tenets--brotherly love, relief and truth. What about twelve? Mackey writes that there are "twelve signs of the zodiac; twelve months in the year, twelve Tribes of Israel; twelve stones in the pectoral or breastplate of the High Priest; and twelve oxen supporting the molten sea in the Temple. There were twelve apostles in the new law, and the New Jerusalem has twelve gates [and] twelve foundations."[1] This is not intended to state that Freemasonry is directly descended from any ancient tradition but rather that the authors of Masonic ritual in the seventeenth, eighteenth, and nineteenth centuries were fully aware of enlightened esoteric ideas and symbolism as expressed in literature especially *The Bible*.

Why, though, do even the ruffians eventually confess? Because truth is a founding principle of the Fraternity and the search for Hiram and the lost word is a metaphor or trope for the search for truth. Not only do we seek the "truth" of who killed Hiram, the ritual also guides us as we seek to understand his fate and his faith. Each Freemason, at some point, is asked to represent Hiram Abiff and to demonstrate, symbolically, at first, and then throughout his life, his integrity. Throughout the degrees all involved engage in a range of allegories and allusions, many of which focus on geometry, the basic and most expansive metaphor of the Fraternity. And while each of the three degrees represents a rite of passage, it is in the Master Mason Degree that this rite is finalized.

The Hiramic Legend was preceded in Masonic Ritual by the Legend of Noah (see Chapter VII). Lamech, the great, great, great, grandson (6th generation) of Adam had two wives and four children: sons Jabal, founder of geometry and builder of the first stone house; Jubal, a musician and founder of music; Tubal, the first blacksmith and worker in brass; and a daughter, Naamah, the founder of weaving. These four erected a pillar of marble and a pillar of brick on which they inscribed on each side the mysteries of their crafts and sciences so that those mysteries would be preserved after the flood. Noah's great grandson, Nimrod, finds the marble pillar and the knowledge thereon contained is imparted to mankind.

The *Graham Manuscript*, however, adds to the legend a form of prequel. After Noah's death, Shem, Ham and Japheth, go to their father's grave in search of a valuable secret. They find nothing but a "dead body all most consumed." Shem, taking the body by a finger and the finger coming off, says "here is yet marrow in this bone." Ham, taking the body by the hand, which also comes off, says "but a dry bone." Japheth then says "it stinketh." They then proceed to raise the body by the elbow supporting it foot-to-foot, knee-to-knee, breast-to-breast, cheek-to-cheek, and hand to back, and cry out "Help O Father." "And so," states the manuscript, "they agreed for to give it a name that is known to freemasonry to this day."[2]

Both the Legend of Noah and, in terms of Masonic Ritual, its successor, the Hiramic Legend, involve a search for something that is lost—a valuable secret. In both legends there is the suggestion that what was lost is the key to special knowledge or light. This aspect of the quest for knowledge is central to virtually all heroic legends and myths to include those of the Holy Grail. All such quests for light are, psychologists suggest, performed in Freemasonry as a circumambulation which symbolizes a search for self. The unconscious is stirred by the journey to seek solutions to problems. The secret is always difficult, if not impossible to find, and the quest is bequeathed to future generations. High virtue is implied and the overall journey represents a major stage in human development: no longer satisfied with just the material, man seeks something higher. These journeys in search of a "secret" seldom reach a satisfactory conclusion, but neither are they misguided. No journey is a straight line and meaning comes through the journey itself not at its destination.

Consider the Grail Legend as an example and Perceval as a craftsman seeking light. Perceval asks questions; finds value in the answers received; and comes to a fuller understanding of his surroundings and circumstances. In the Arthurian legend, the ultimate question is "Whom does the Grail serve?" The goal of Perceval's quest is the end of the old and the beginning of the new. The question is no longer "Whom does the Grail serve?", but rather "what purpose does the initiate's journey serve?" The Noah Legend, the Hiramic Legend, and the Grail Legend do not impart direct knowledge, rather they teach us about our readiness to receive enlightenment. Carl Jung writes in *Memories, Dreams, Reflections* that "I myself am a question."[3] The great Masonic legend teaches us, through ritual, to listen to our inner selves and to be reflective, thus not allowing ourselves to become bedazzled or distracted during our quest. There is also a hint in all three degrees of Freemasonry, as there is in the character of Gawain in the Grail Legend, of the need to take time for personal reflection and inner self. While outer events were critical, it is internal reflection that proved vital for Gawain, Perceval, and the Fellow Crafts.

To come to an understanding of how a legend grows and transmutes into both accepted history and ritual, we will consider the Legend of King Arthur noted above. Arthur is described as a British leader of the fifth or sixth century who led the native people in their defense against the invading Saxons. Early references to the character may be found in *Historia Brittonum* which is of Welsh origin and was written about 828 and traces British history to survivors of Troy, and in the mid tenth century *Annales Cambriae (Annals of Wales)* complied also in Wales with the earliest extant version being a twelfth century copy. There is, however, no mention of Arthur in *The Cryoland Chronicle* (abt. 665), Bede's *Ecclesiastical History of the English People* (eight century), or *The Anglo Saxon Chronicles* (ninth century). It must be kept in mind that Arthur was of Welsh origin and the Welsh, severely oppressed by their English neighbors, were in need of a mighty national hero. In the 1130s, however, an Oxford scholar named Geoffrey of Monmouth created out of a few obscure references found in Welsh sources the most brilliant and enduring legend of the Middle Ages if not all history—King Arthur. In his book *The History of the Kings of Britain*, which does contain sufficient scraps of legitimate history to make it appear credible, Geoffrey recounts the exploits of Arthur and declares him the greatest of all Britons and, at one time, "ruler of the world."[4] And even though William of Newburgh writing about fifty years later declared these exploits as "made up," by the time of Edward I in the mid thirteenth century, Arthur had become as real a historical person as Edward the Confessor, William the Conqueror, and Richard I, all of whom were Edward's ancestors.

Geoffrey's *History* was a bestseller in its day and more than 215 manuscript copies still survive, second only to *The Bible* in term of extant medieval English texts. Arthur was quickly given a magnificent castle—Camelot, a host of companions (some of who betrayed him), and a Round Table. And by 1185 he had a tomb at Glastonbury Abbey. When the Abbey burned in 1184, the resident monks, utilizing an early form of creative marketing, "discovered", buried in their cemetery, not only Arthur, but also Guinevere, interred under an inscribed lead cross. A motivating force in the "finding" of the long-interred remains was Henry II, Edward's grandfather who, for his own reasons, wanted Arthur dead and buried. In 1278 Edward I returned to Glastonbury in the spring not only because he and his wife were Arthurian enthusiasts and true believers, but also to reinter the raised remains at the Abbey where, eventually, a magnificent black marble tomb was constructed with a lion at each end, and an image of Arthur at the foot. The legend gave rise to plays, rituals, tournaments, pageants, books, movies, and, even, a fraternity.

For Edward I the Legend of Arthur was integral to his kingdom and to the chivalric beliefs of his followers. It also linked British royalty to the great Roman Emperor Constantine. In 1284 Edward again traveled into Wales and "discovered" the interred remains of Emperor Maximus, the Western Roman Emperor who ruled Britannia and Gaul beginning about 384. Maximus, according to legend, was the father of Constantine who brought Christianity to the Roman Empire and, according to Geoffrey, the grandfather of Arthur. [5]

The Legend of Arthur and its accompanying ceremonies were political ritual and theatre at its highest and served to unite the community around a commonly believed legend. It even led one of Edward's supporters to invest vast sums in the renovation of the remote Tintagel where Arthur is said to have been conceived. It further led to mock battles in the form of "Round Table" tournaments with an emphasis on jousting, pageantry, and chivalry performed ritualistically in a manner that furthered the transmission not only of the legend and national or group identity, but also the moral lessons inherent in the story of Arthur and the quest for the Grail.

The Hiramic Legend and its accompanying ritual followed a similar path. The name "Hiram" first appears in I Kings and II Samuel. Yet as Coil notes "There is no reference to Hiram in any of the Gothic Constitutions, and those to Solomon and his Temple are of the briefest character."[6] In Anderson's *Constitutions of 1723* there is mention of the character, but by 1738 it is evident that the Legend had become significantly more developed and was by that time an integral part of Masonic tradition and practice. Further expansion and explanation of the legend was given by The Reverend Dr. George Oliver and, in later generations, many other Masonic writers. And as the Legend developed, so too did the ritual that utilized the Legend as its basic allegory. Coil includes in his entry on Hiram that there are numerous theories about the source of the legend to include an allusion to the legend of Osiris; an allegory of the expulsion from Eden; the death and resurrection of Christ; the persecution of the Templars; the death of Charles I of England coupled with a Jacobite myth invented to aid the House of Stuart; and, even, a similar invention of Oliver Cromwell to aid him in his fight against that very House of Stuart. Coil further notes, and probably more accurately, that the Legend of Hiram is "an appropriate little drama to make a stirring ritualistic ceremony."[7] But as noted elsewhere in this text, the Hiramic Legend, as with the Arthur legend, is allegorical teaching at its highest providing those who penetrate its veil sound instruction on the perils of human frailty as well as the importance of a man's integrity. It may be a legend as is the story of Arthur, but Hiram and Arthur have much to teach us about how to live in the modern age.

Of course, defining ritual is not an easy task. Sometimes we feel that it is something real, but hard to verbalize. At other times we perceive it as an artificial construct. It is most often defined in its religious context as "a manner for performing divine services;" in its ceremonial function as "a body or code of ceremonies;" and psychologically as "an often repeated series of actions." It is repetitive, stylized, and symbolic, as previously noted. It also tends to be culturally standardized and is generally perceived as a combination of words and actions. It communicates ideas and leads to group cohesion. And while it is often "fun"—a wedding, for example—it can also be extremely serious such as at a funeral. Above all, ritual involves a paradox. A paradox is something that might be true but might not. It appears to teach one lesson, when it may actually teach another. The Legend of Arthur on the surface is a tale of a quest for a sacred object. It is far more, however, and is, upon close analysis, a full allegory for the human quest for knowledge and fulfillment. The Legend of Hiram, likewise, appears on the surface to be a story of trust, betrayal, and retribution. But again, it is an allegory in its truest sense of man's quest for his own integrity as well as for enlightenment. Both utilize expressive characters to communicate in a manner that, through action, get things done.

Rites of passage, according to Arnold van Gennep, "accompany every change of place, state, social position, and age"[8] and utilize symbolic behavior to signify a detachment from an earlier stage and a new beginning. These rites take the individual from a state of pre-ritual stability through a period of instability—the rituals or rites themselves—into a relatively new stable state of being. In this new state, the initiate is expected to adhere to certain cultural or organizational norms and ethical standards thus ensuring himself a position in the hierarchy of the group and a place in the system. The neophyte or candidate is represented as possessing nothing—being in darkness—with no status, insignia, or distinctive clothing. He is expected to behave in a passive and humble manner following the directions of his conductor or guide and "fearing no danger" while expressing high levels of humility. By being reduced of external trappings—clothing, jewelry, and the like—they are prepared to be endowed with new accoutrements symbolic of their membership in the community or Fraternity.

Initiates tend to develop strong comradeship with other initiates that are generally egalitarian. Secular distinctions of race, class, education, and outward appearance disappear and they become part of a *communitas*. This model of human interaction tends to bind the group into one distinct band which endeavors to meets the goals of the group rather than the goals of the individual. The hierarchal system disappears within the group (though one member may, by strength of personality, be perceived as the leader) and group endeavors become paramount. In some cultures, and societies, this "community" is enforced by separating the initiates from the larger group for some period of time; time that is usually devoted to instruction and reflection. The group tends not only to study together, but to socialize together as it bonds.

This process, suggests Victor Turner, is essential to human bonding and "without it there can be no society."[9] Consider in this light the actions of many members of European royalty such as Prince Philip in England who send their sons and grandsons to various bush or pioneer schools so that they may learn to "rough it" while becoming more egalitarian in their social bonding. There has also been among the British Royal Family a tendency toward military service with serves the same egalitarian purpose. A significant part of the typical initiation ritual or training, therefore, involves instruction in self-mastery; the role of the initiate and the group in the society; and an introduction to group rites, norms, attitudes, and relationships. Sacred wisdom is imparted to the initiate. The candidate, who was, essentially, a blank slate prior to the ceremony, is now "inscribed" with the wisdom and knowledge of the group. He is introduced to relationships and kinships within the group and understands his position in that society.

In western culture, the binding of a community such as that accomplished through the Rule of St. Benedict "provides for the life of men who wish to live in community . . . they are essentially families whose common vows distinguish them from secular life."[10] In western society *communitas* or community is to be noted among several groups, especially the fraternities and societies such as Freemasons, Odd Fellows, Elks, and Moose. There are also indicators of a similar community status among veterans' organizations, but that community is based more on a previous shared experience—military service—rather than on ritualistic initiation into the organization. Within a *communitas*, structure is often rooted soundly in the past but extends into the present and future through language, ritual, symbolism, law, and custom.

All initiation rituals or rites of passage involve specified age limits. In the Jewish faith, the age of thirteen establishes a person as a "son of the commandments" or a "daughter of the commandments." Heretofore, their parents were responsible for their actions. At age thirteen the initiate assumes that responsibility. The parents can no longer be punished for the sins of their children. Within early medieval Christian societies, age twelve was generally deemed the "age of adulthood" with marriage and the resulting consummation legalized by the Church. Through succeeding generations, the age of adulthood or responsibility slowly crept forward or receded. In eighteenth century Freemasonry the age of initiation was age twenty-five. Subsequent generations reduced the age to twenty-one, and in many jurisdictions, the age has now been lowered to eighteen. At issue, of course, is the lack of a clear definition of "age of responsibility" which varies from nation to nation and from culture to culture.

Communities may be formed on three bases: spontaneous, normative, and ideological. A spontaneous community arises from an agreed upon event or "happening" in which a group meets and then disperses. A normative community is formed under the influence of time to mobilize resources to address a perceived need. These communities generally focus on some form of social control or address a social issue. Ideological communities are those societies which focus on existential concerns or attempts to define human existence. Freemasonry fits into this last definition. Each community establishes its own rules and structures, and tends to use imagery to transmit meanings. A central focus of many communities is the conveyance of explicit views on how men may best live together in harmony; how they can work hard, work together, and agree at the same. A community is not, however, a utopia and may not therefore be perfect. It is composed of individuals each with their own agenda, motive, and reward system.

Communities—and fraternities such as Freemasonry are communities—focus on the *we* rather than the *me*. Relationships within the group are paramount with members often assigning specific honorifics to each other such as "Brother," "Worshipful," "Comrade," or "Compatriot." The concept of *we* within a community is intended to prevent a person who is greedy for power from using the others in the group to his own ends. The *we* in a fraternity tends to isolate those who crave importance only without making a marked contribution to the group. Communities tend also to follow the "all for one and one for all philosophy" and are often influenced by a legend of a great leader or a person worthy of emulation. The Franciscan Order within the Catholic Church along with Freemasonry are examples of this trend. St. Francis endeavored to live, and encouraged others to live, in terms of certain views of poverty and service to mankind. In a similar manner, the Freemason's legend of Hiram Abiff provides guidance on how to live and how to perform under duress.

The transmission of thought or ideas in a community or fraternity tends to be done symbolically as the group grows larger. St. Francis often described his ideas not as words but as images leaping from one picture to another. When he sought to explain his rule to Pope Innocent III, he turned to a parable in much the same manner that Jesus did when explaining his thoughts to his disciples. Parables are symbolic thought and utilize abstractions to make a point or transmit meaning. St. Francis, for example, described his decision to resign his position as head of the order in terms of a "little red hen" who was too small to cover her chicks with her wings. In a similar manner the Knights Templar, faced with an organization that extended from beyond the middle-east spreading throughout Europe to include

England and Scotland, developed an extensive "rule" which eventually included six hundred and eighty-five (685) detailed paragraphs clarifying their mission. This codification, however, moved the Templars from the spiritual to the conventional, from the symbolic to the structural.

As an organization grows, it develops the tools essential to governance and continuity. Divisions in jurisdiction are established each with its designated territory and authority. In Freemasonry outside the United States there tend to be national Grand Lodges. In England, for example, the United Grand Lodge of England or U.G.L.E. currently has about eight thousand Lodges organized into Provincial Grand Lodges which were approximately equivalent to the historic counties of England. These include the Metropolitan Grand Lodge of London, headed by the Metropolitan Grand Master, Provincial Grand Lodges (U.G.L.E.) headed by a Provincial Grand Master, District Grand Lodges headed by a District Grand Master, and five groups currently too small to be formal districts headed by a Grand Inspector. There are also U.G.L.E. units in many Commonwealth Nations or nations that were once part of that organization. Within the United States, Grand Lodges are defined by states and include the District of Columbia and Puerto Rico. Each Grand Lodge is presided over by an elected Grand Master. Each U.S. Grand Lodge is further divided into geographical districts supervised by a District Deputy Grand Master, District Lecturer, or similar officer appointed by the Grand Master.

Grand Lodges, and in turn, individual Lodges, administer the Fraternity and exercise legislative, disciplinary, and election functions. They also perpetuate the history and principles of the Craft through approved ritual which utilizes agreed upon meaning and symbolism to transmit information. And, as within all human endeavors, there is some degree of rivalry similar to that expressed between the Dominicans and the Franciscans, but such rivalry is fraternal in nature rather than punitive. In the United States, this friendly rivalry is expressed most commonly in differences in ritual practices and some symbolic meaning with the greater principles of the Fraternity remaining intact and universal.

Within the ritual environment, some proponents are deemed devotionalists and others conservatives. Devolutionalists focus primarily on meaning while conservatives tend to focus on instruction and action. A similar dichotomy may be found in the major monotheistic religions: Christianity, Judaism, and Islam. Devotionalists suggest that the path to knowledge is through reflection and meditation while conservatives are more active and less passive. The nature of Masonic ritual lends itself to the conservative rather than the devotional approach with its inherent concept being that actions based upon understanding obtained through reflection and study lead to enlightenment.

Van Gennep, who is also considered the "father of processual analysis," emphasizes the structural aspects of rites of passage and initiations. Structure in this regard is accepted to mean the social structures that are imparted to the initiates through myth, allegory, and ritual. One of the most common symbols used in initiation is the life crisis. The candidate is "leveled" and undergoes a series of tests to teach humanity, humility, and obedience. The implication is clear; in order to advance to a higher level, the candidate must first go lower. He must be humbled before being elevated.

Rituals of status reversal or leveling serve to affirm the structure and order of the organization and, in turn, society in general. The student who was a mighty high school senior becomes a lowly college freshman only to be elevated again through the academic journey and a search for knowledge which may take years. The military officer who enters airborne school becomes a lowly candidate and no longer enjoys his command position which will be resumed at the end of the quest. Upon completion of the ritual experience in Freemasonry, however. the individual assumes a new role which may not match his position in life outside the organization. When Brothers Theodore and Franklin Roosevelt attended Lodge, they were not addressed as Mr. President, but rather as Brother. And Brother Harry Truman was, in sequence, Brother Harry Truman, then Worshipful Harry Truman, and finally Most Worshipful Harry Truman before becoming Mr. President. But he remained throughout his life after initiation, above all, Brother Harry. They met upon the level. The *communitas* was confirmed as was their place in it.

Directly associated with initiation rituals is the power of mutual honesty and its place in the social structure. Humility is also a virtue in a fraternal society and patience is rewarded. The expression of honesty, humility, and patience manifests itself in the stress placed upon a mystical union between the initiate and the fraternity as well as in a reduction in external distinctions of status, age, property, or physical attributes. Many religious and fraternal organizations have been founded by individuals of relatively high social or structural standing. Humility is perceived not as the final goal but rather as an attribute necessary to further progress. The Buddha, for example, was an individual who was politically and by lineage well endowed, yet through humility he became the equal of his followers. In the Christian Catholic tradition, we find Saints Benedict, Dominic, and Clare. In the Protestant tradition may be found George Fox, Alexander Campbell, and the Wesley brothers. All of these were influential yet humble and perceived their service as being to the community rather than to themselves.

Rituals and rites of initiation are typically cyclically repetitive with the same ritual being performed again and again. This repetition is necessary for learning and, in complex societies, serves to strengthen the ties that bind the members of the community together. Tribal communities in less developed nations also demonstrate the community strengthening property of repeated ritual. Society, however, is not a thing, it is a process. Humans have a "need" to belong and to participate in a community. Humans also have a desire to achieve. All humans tend to aspire to become more than they are and ritual provides the means. The United States Army uses "be all that you can be" as a motto. Freemasonry offers the motto "making good men better" through our symbolic community, our ritual, and our fellowship.

What is accomplished through ritual is the creation of order and control in a world filled with flux, chaos, and entropy. Ritual addresses issues of irregularity while at the same time giving disorder its due by keeping it within specific boundaries. The ultimate goal is community coherence and celebration of the same. Ritual is a collective function that celebrates the sense of awe achieved through teamwork. It meets the intrinsic human need to belong and establishes boundaries which define the group. Groups tend to need ritual to create and maintain themselves because it reinforces shared values and demonstrates group expectations. It provides assumptions about daily life which can be acted upon outside the ritual. In life, repeated action leads to automatic responses. But you cannot instill values such as loyalty, honor, and truthfulness through rote recitation. These values are learned through examples and allegories which are inherent to ritual. With the establishment of values and the accompanying process of revising one's vision of his place in society comes also the recognition that there is now a separation between the previous state and the new state. Ritual has enabled us to "move on."

Ritual also performs the task of identifying and naming things, but the performance must be persuasive if it is to be effective. A priest is consecrated and not only become a different person, he now has a new identity--"Father." A man and woman engage in a wedding ceremony and the minister pronounces them "man and wife together" declaring them a couple, and in most such ceremonies, the woman assumes a new identity by taking on the last name of her husband while the husband assumes a new identify as an individual joined legally and morally to another. A prince is anointed with holy oil and receives the new identity of king. All of these are examples of ritual at work transforming (initiating) and persuading with the spectators, ritualists, and participants accepting fully the new identity achieved.

The assumption is often made that all rituals are good; that they are good for the society which practices them; and that they function for the good of and within that group. These assumptions are not always valid. Some rituals, such as those of kingship, essentially benefit only one person—the king. Others simply enforce the status quo which benefits only the more senior generations. While others, such as rituals of power, benefit only the politically elite. But as previously noted, ritual often deals with questions of contradictions and social problems. They teach us that life is not consistent and is often fraught with danger. In industrialized, institutionalized societies, ritual serves as an escape valve for social tensions by facilitating the formation of communities. Ritual serves to ease the transition from youth to adulthood; from seeking blindly, to seeking with guidance. And while rituals do this, they also provide pleasure and fulfillment through collective effort.

Masonic ritual goes further by providing a narrative that involves an archetypical figure who demonstrates compassion, truthfulness, knowledge, and integrity. The narrative is not literally true and even contains some discrepancies (as do all legends), but it is a useful teaching tool. The narrative encourages us to "become upset with" bad behavior and endeavor to imitate the "great" and the "good." The ritual narrative sets the limits or circumscribes the boundaries beyond which we venture at our own peril. The story of Hiram, the narrative of the Third Degree, encourages us to question our actions and to establish for ourselves the value of our integrity.

NOTES

1. Albert G. Mackey and Charles Thompson. *An Encyclopedia of Freemasonry and Its Kindred Sciences.* (Philadelphia: Louis Everts, 1905), 838.

2. Anonymous. *The Graham Manuscript.* Abt. 1724. Located at www.omdhs.syracusemasons.com/sites/default/files/philosopy/Graham%20ms/%20-%208%20pt%20copy.pdf. Retrieved January 9, 2016.

3. C.G Jung and Aniela Jaffee. *Memories, Dreams, Reflections.* (New York: Knopf Doubleday, 1965), 350.

4. Lewis Thorpe, Ed. *Geoffrey of Monmouth, History of the Kings of Britain.* (Guild: London, 1966), 9.

5. Edward I created an eighteen feet in diameter Round Table at Winchester Castle about 1275. The table weighs three-quarters of a ton, had a center support, and twelve legs. The table is make of solid English oak. It has hung on a wall at the Castle since at least 1560. Henry VIII had the table repainted to depict himself as King Arthur.

6. Henry W. Coil. *Coil's Masonic Encyclopedia.* (New York: Macoy Publishing & Masonic Supply Company, 1961), 307.

7. Coil, *Coil's Magazine,* 309.

8. Victor W. Turner. *The Forest of Symbols.* (Ithaca, NY: Cornell University Press, 1967), 93-111.

9. Victor Turner. *The Ritual Process: Structure and Anti-Structure.* (New Brunswick, Conn.: Aldine Transaction, 2008), 97.

10. Donald Attwater (ed.). *A Catholic Dictionary.* (New York: Macmillan0, 1961, 51.

Chapter Four

Ritual Architecture

That is how architecture is to be known. As the material theatre of human activity, its truth is in its use.
Spiro Kostof

The cave art of Europe and Asia was considered by many to be the earliest form of ritual architecture dating from between 25,000 and 30,000 B.C.E., but French archeologists following up on a 1990s discovery of mysterious Paleolithic circles in Bruniquel Cave located in the southwestern part of that country have now been reported in *Nature, National Geographic,* and *Science Magazine* [1] the confirmed existence of stone structures constructed predominately from stalagmites crafted into large circles measuring nearly twenty-two feet in diameter. These circles, located some 1,000 feet inside the cave, have been dated to about 177,000 years ago using advanced radioactive-dating techniques. The structures display what researchers (archeologists, anthropologists, and paleontologists) agree is evidence of human planning and activity and, based upon the date, are considered evidence of deliberate construction by Neanderthals, cousins of modern humans.

Neanderthal and modern human DNA are 99.5% the same and there is, within modern human DNA, evidence of interbreeding with Neanderthals. And while there are hints that Neanderthals, who existed between 600,000 and 28,000 years ago, may have built structures above ground, the stone circles are the only remaining Neanderthal-related deliberate structures still visible. Considering the location of the circles some 1,000 feet from the cave's entrance; the lack of residue suggesting long-term habitation; and the striking geometric shape (a typical ritual formation), it is possible that these very ancient constructions represent the first ritual sites created by a human predecessor or relative. If this contention is confirmed by further research, these stone circles--possibly ritual structures--would suggest that ritual activity was an integral part of the earliest human thought patterns. And, based on the work of Perreault and Mathew in dating the origin of human language, could place the development of ritual parallel with the development that uniquely human activity which flowed seamlessly into the development of modern humans some 100,000 years later.

Ritualization, therefore, appears to be an innate human activity far predating any modern conception of religion or public activity. It is essential to our perception of our world and our place in it as well as our understanding of our internal selves and our relationships to external events and concepts. Ritual may, therefore, be among those few things that truly define us as human and, as such, was and is essential to the success of our species past, present, and future.

The oldest megalithic architecture which is confirmed as a ritual structure is found at Gobekli Tepe in southern Turkey and was built about eleven thousand years ago (9000 B.C.E.) some 166,000 years after the creation of the Bruniquel Cave circles but predating the Great Pyramid of Giza (about. 2650 B.C.E.) and Stonehenge (possibly as early as (about 3400 B.C.E.) by many millennia. Its pillars, the tallest of which is eighteen feet high weighing about sixteen tons, are made of limestone and heavily incised or engraved with geometric shapes, images similar to men, and a variety of reptiles, insects, and mammals. The pillars are nested in concentric circles which appear to form enclosures. To date, more than two hundred of the finely

Figure 4.1.   Bruniquel Cave, France. © Michel SOULIER/SSAC + CNRS.

Figure 4.2. Lascaux Cave Paintings, France.

hewn pillars have been unearthed along with the remains of walls and benches.

Gobekli Tepe was not primarily a burial site nor was it a city, any more than was Stonehenge. The people who performed their rituals there walked several miles just to visit. It was, Klaus Schmidt, a lead investigator at the site notes: "first a temple. . . [and] a religious sanctuary."[2] Its principle use was as a ritual center, not as a settlement. The traditional cultural narrative has been that hunter-gathers transition into agriculturally based, permanent communities with the corresponding establishment of a division of labor, social status, and hierarchies. When community life became more settled, the original theory suggested, religious life and ritual followed. Research at Gobekli Tepe and recent analysis of even more ancient cave paintings and structures suggest otherwise. A new interpretation of the archeological records suggests, instead, that ritual sites themselves may have been instrumental in the establishment of communities, not the other way around. At Gobekli Tepe, Schmidt interprets the evidence to say that large groups of possibly nomadic foragers came together to build the massive complex and this construction, in turn, created a focal point for a more permanent, agricul-

Figure 4.3. Gobekli Tepe, Turkey.

turally based society. The structures at Gobekli Tepe are clearly not domestic in nature and appear to have had no practical function. The site is a sanctuary, not a home.

In other words, at Gobekli Tepe and other ritual sites, the structures do not directly serve the community other than as sites for communal gatherings with their accompanying feasting, storytelling, singing, and ritual. The sites were, for those who participated in ritual there, a bridge between the natural and the spiritual world. They were forerunners of Delphi and attracted wayfarers from the surrounding countryside. They were separate spaces dedicated to ritual: places for ritual to take place. Jonathan Z. Smith goes further and suggests that action becomes ritual by virtue of its placement. Ritual is not ordinary, Smith notes, and thus requires a "nonordinary" locale. Ritual is significant and symbolic requiring, therefore, that great care must be taken to perform ritual in dedicated sacred spaces.

Ritual has many components and, formal or informal, may appear ordinary and domestic. To be clear, ritual is more about the action than the space, but in early communities, space appears to be integral to the satisfactory performance of ritual. Dualism is a characteristic of modern Western thought and is not an ancient concept. It suggests that ritual may now be performed as easily in the kitchen as in the sanctuary. It is still accepted, however, that ritual performed at dedicated sites or in special settings achieves a higher

Figure 4.4.   Giza Plateau, Egypt.

aesthetic and emotional level with an accompanying greater impact on participants and viewers. If this were not the case even in the twenty-first century,
there would be no need for churches or other liturgical spaces; no dedicated
burial grounds; and, for that matter, no sports stadiums or entertainment
venues. Each of these represents a space dedicated to a particular form of
community ritual, which, like politics with its dedicated spaces, is considered
essential to societal success.

An altar, an architectural element, is the most common structure used in
ritual. It symbolizes an integration, a pivot point, between the self and the
universe. It is the central point- of-focus for the event. It is usually elevated
so that all can see it and, when used by the ritualist, the high point allows for
an unobstructed view of the surroundings, the participants, and the spectators. It is the axis along which the guiding light of the Deity comes to man.
An altar is a central pillar both for the participant and the viewer and an
anchor for emotions, reactions, and reflection. Altars originally may have
represented the point at which something emerged from nothing symbolically or realistically. They may represent the navel of the earth; the place where
water first sprang forth from barren ground or where a tree sprout first
appeared in rocky soil. They may even locate the site where God appeared to
man or where an angel became visible.

In European cathedrals, the altar commonly represents the Tomb of Christ
and is thus highly symbolic of the relationship between man and God. Altars
are usually covered with a cloth and are the resting place for sacred texts and
symbols. Altars are usually oriented east and west to represent, anciently, the

Figure 4.5.   Stonehenge, Salisbury Plain, England.

four elements, and in Hebrew, Christian, and Masonic iconography, the first Tabernacle. This orientation anciently appears to be directly related to the observable fact that the sun rises in the east and sets in the west with some altars being oriented not only to the east but also to the rising sun on a specific day—the solstice. Some western churches are still oriented so that the sun on Easter Sunday morning will enter the main doors and stream down the aisle to illuminate the altar thus symbolizing the resurrection. Though it must be noted that the dating of Easter in the Christian tradition makes precision in this matter difficult

All ritual architecture, especially altars, are manifestations of what the participant needs to feel during the event. The most common expectation are feelings of awe and reverence. Architecture effects the human mind, writes John Ruskin, and ritual is the poetry that makes the functional piece symbolic. Architecture enhances the mystery of ritual. The great Hagia Sophia in Istanbul, Turkey, "sings the ineffableness of Christian mystery in providing a space of which one user is man and the other user is unseen and unpredictable"[3] , man and God in a single space. Architecture, Kostof continues, does not, however, always reflect every aspect of human endeavor or social order. It is a useful art in that it prepares the stage on which humans perform. The pyramids of the Giza Plateau molded the social mores of Egyptian society as much as they reflected an interpretation of the power of the Pharaoh. They, and the accompanying funeral complexes and temples, created the impression sought as much as they facilitated the transmittal of the myth of the deity. Architecture is a medium of cultural expression to the extent that through it we are able to process and understand the message. The consistent question in ritual architecture, in all architecture for that matter, is "what does it mean?"

Architecture is a means for establishing boundaries and therefore implies human intervention. It is also indicative of man's desire to shape his environment rather than allow the environment to shape man. Caves are nature's architecture, but they come ready made and do not always conform to man's needs. Early man adapted them to his use by installing sleeping platforms, fire rings, and placing coverings over the entrances. The earliest human encampment not nature-made dates to about 400,000 years ago and is located in Terra Amata near Monte Carlo. These were purposeful structures made of branches or saplings set in the dirt or sand. As building technology advanced over the next 300,000 years or so, ritual use of architecture followed. The first huts were reinforced and weather-proofed with animal skins and thus weatherized. The most formable foe of ancient man was the weather, and as the hunter-gatherer began to attempt to control this aspect of the environment, he established rites to appease the gods and to assure his own destiny. The shelter became more than mere housing; it also became a sanctuary.

Figure 4.6.   Roman Forum, Italy.

Accompanying this advancement in architecture, came a similar advancement in art. Tools, murals, engravings, and sculptures arose as expressions of thoughts and the image became more than that which was depicted. Ritual transformed the cave and then the hut into something with hidden meaning requiring interpretation.

Ritual architecture abounds worldwide. There are caves in France and Indonesia; temples in Malta, Mycenae, and Minoan cities; standing stones in Germany and England; even more temples and tombs in Egypt; classical structures in Greece and Rome; and Romanesque, Norman, and Gothic cathedrals dot the European landscape. Many of these, like Stonehenge, were designed to plot and predict solar alignments. But that is the function of the structure, not its meaning. The calendar could easily have been done, and was done, on a much smaller scale. It could even be held in the hand as suggested by the Nebra sky disk. The phenomenal engineering feat and the intense, protracted labor involved, didn't just create a "Neolithic computer," they created a sacred center for community activities of initiation and renewal. This is public architecture at its best. It enhances ritual which results in the participants becoming something more than they previously were.

Stonehenge, located on the Salisbury Plain in southern England, is perhaps the best known Neolithic ritual structure in Europe. Its blue stones were originally thought to have been set in place between 2,400 and 2,200 B.C.E. though earlier work at the site is dated to about 3,100 B.C.E. Research reported in 2015, however, shows evidence that the dramatic blue stones were cut from rocky outcrops at Carn Goedog and Craig Rhos-y-felin in Wales around 3,400 B.C.E. and transported more than 140 miles to their current site not arriving at Stonehenge until about 2,900 B.C.E., some 500 years later. The Carn Goedog site shows similar stones cut from the crag that were left behind and nearby are what appears to be "loading bays" for use in dragging the stone from the site. This evidence suggests that Stonehenge is at least 500 years older than originally thought and that "the stones were first used in a local monument, somewhere near the quarries, that was then dismantled and dragged off to Wiltshire."[4]

The long distance transport of these eighty monoliths demonstrates that the structure served to bring people together from distance parts of England to ritualistically move the sacred monument from its original site to its current location. Ritualistic journeys and the coordination necessary to the success of ritual are significant parts of the experience and include not only short circumambulations around the Lodge room or the cathedral but also the 140-mile trek taking some 500 years ago dragging the four-ton stones from Wales to Wiltshire. This is ritual architecture at its most compelling and impressive, and indicates mankind's strong attachment to ritual practices.

As times, regimens, and religions changed, so too did their accompanying architecture. Egypt is a prime example of this evolution. When Amenhotep

IV and Akhenaten attempted to replace the old religion with a sun-disk cult, the revolt was short-lived. The brief period was highlighted, however, by the construction of Amarna between Upper and Lower Egypt. Upon Akhenaten's death and the restoration of the god Amon, the new city and its temple were razed. What is most interesting, however, is that Egyptian ritual architecture in general changed little over millennia. New Kingdom temples utilized architectural features such as columns very similar to those of the Old Kingdom, and even under foreign invaders including the Greek Ptolemaist, the restrained, stately architecture of Egypt survived. The very rhythms and nature of faith and practice were permanent with the buildings transcending time and authorship.

Imperial Rome also witnessed ritual architecture in its highest form. The Roman Forum lent itself to public ritual and during the reign of Nero, the Golden House became the ideal official residence for a Roman ruler. It was a stage for ritual ceremonies as much as it was the Emperor's residence. The ruler received clients with ritualistic formality, dispensed justice, and dined with peers. These relatively mundane governmental activities achieved the level of an operatic performance. Nothing was too ostentatious for the Emperor. Subsequent Emperors expanded the imperial city and its ritual spaces to include a series of imperial forums, possibly the greatest architectural projects in antiquity. Mighty civic centers were created that accommodated

Figure 4.7. Hagia Sophia, Turkey.

not only governmental ritual and function, but also military triumphs and a wide range of public performances. The remaining center-piece of this mighty city is the Colosseum used for both imperial rites and bloody sacrifice.

As the Roman Empire reached its zenith internally, it expanded externally stretching from the British Isles in the northeast to the Limes Germanicus in modern Eastern Europe to the Euphrates in the east and south to include Egypt and the Arabian Peninsula. The material used in imperial architecture ranged from earth to basalt, tile, concrete, and native stone. It was the duty of the architect to spread the collective existence which defined Rome. Edifices and architecture as well as city planning were intended to provide a suitable stage for public and governmental rites and rituals. With the demise of Rome, which began in the mid fourth century and ended over one hundred years later, there was a marked end to major architectural projects in the West and with that a severe reduction in ritual expression. The Emperor Justinian died in 565 and with him went his dream of restoring Roman glory. Cities fell into decay and civic structures were savaged for building materials for common houses. The geometric, well-planned complexity of early forms was replaced with a relatively piece-meal system of civic organization. Ritual and ritual structures suffered the same fate.

During the centuries between 410 (the final fall of the City of Rome) and rebirth of Europe in the tenth and eleventh centuries, new structures were primarily religious with a strong focus on monastic life and seclusion. Defense became paramount and towers dotted the countryside as well as the settlements and walled enclosures became common. And though stone architecture with it requisite skill level and planning did not die out, severely simplified Roman forms such as the arch and vault predominated, usually composed of a combination of wood and brick or stone. Basilica churches were common in Western Europe even though the form had been discarded in the East after Justinian. Western ritual architecture was expressed in terms of the ritual itself: simple and solid. An unpretentious rectangular hall flanked by small appendages such as an apse, choir, or tower became common. The main hall was entered through small doors only—no grand entry as would be found later in Gothic cathedrals. In a few of these structures, low cross arms appeared near the altar which would evolve into the transect.

Daily liturgical ritual defined the architecture with the focus being on Mass. In the monasteries, the walls, porticoes, and enclosed spaces provided for an environment in which services were continuous and even circumambulations were well defined and purposeful. The monastery and the church provided for quiet contemplation and gave all involved the opportunity to revere their surroundings as they contemplated their faith and their reason for being. The ritual architecture presented the participant a symbolic representation of God's relationship to his creatures and established the power and transcendence of the Deity.

There is no truly typical Romanesque church. There are regional and programmatic differences in what could be considered an international style. The facades of the churches are usually unfinished in sharp contrast with the elaborately decorated gothic cathedrals. But all early Christian churches demonstrate an ideal diagram based on the liturgy. The Abby Church of St. Foy at Conques in France will serve to illustrate the iconography used to match the ritual. The monastery was built in the eight century with the original chapel being destroyed by fire in the eleventh century. It is the repository of the relics St. Foy, a young girl martyred in the fourth century. Her relics arrive at the site in 866. The Abbey was a well-known stop for pilgrims traveling the Way of St. James to Santiago de Compostela in Spain. The total building is an extension of the ritual and thus required functionality. These early churches had to be defensible, as well, and are often adorned with towers that provided not only visibility but also demonstrated status. Some decorative elements were in place during this period to include murals and statuary, often done in high relief and focusing on the Last Judgement. These structures were intended to serve as stations on the pilgrimage through life. And the symbolism incorporated in their spaces demonstrated for the parishioners the character of their faith.

At the top at Conques is the Deity most often represented by a cross surrounded by angels blowing trumpets summoning judgement. In the middle is enthroned Christ floating on a cloud, his right hand raised to heaven, his left pointing down to hell. At his feet are represented the dead being raised from their graves and, after the weighing of their souls, some are led by angels to heaven, others carried away by demons to hell. At the head of the line of those heaven bound is the Virgin Mary followed by St. Peter along with an abbot and a king. The damned include monks, knights, and others confronted by a guardian angel armed with shield and lance. The rich display of symbols coupled with the performance of the ritual provided a pageantry that impressed as it taught. The worshiper who entered this realm was immediately struck by the cosmic drama depicted on the walls and ceiling. And when the symbols were explained through the ritual, a sure and straight path to salvation was clear.

The Romanesque style in the French world was somewhat different, as was the ritual, because it tended to be regional there being no true national boundaries at that time. A prime example of French Romanesque ritual architecture is found at the Abby Church at Cluny, the principal abbey of the Cluniac order which dates to about 1095. The layout of the church proper is in the Benedictine scheme and includes a choir, vestibule, nave, and, later, a cloister. The glory of Cluny was not only in its art, but in its size which accommodated up to 1,200 monks. The building was constructed to provide

Figure 4.8.   Abbey Church St. Foy, France.

Figure 4.9. Tympanum, Abbey Church St. Foy, France.

separate spaces for the celebration of liturgy and the more mundane work of
the monks. At Cluny, and other monasteries, monks no longer "cut ourselves
off from the people. . . in order that we may obtain Christ"[5] as Bernard of
Clairvaux's interpretation of the Benedictine Rule demanded, but rather the
site represents a transformation of a pious, liturgical based community into a
social and community center.

Unlike so many other early Christian churches, the architect of Cluny is
known. His name was Gunzo. He was a cleric or brother well known in his
community as a musician. His training and proficiency in music may well
have contributed directly to his success as an architect. St. Augustine had
written centuries before that music was "the science of good modulation" and
that its very nature was based in mathematics. So, too, is good architecture.
Music is based on ratios: an octave, a fifth, and a fourth—1:2, 2:3, and 3:4.
Architecture is no different. Proportion is the function of geometry and
geometry, like music, is an analog activity. Music and architecture have the
ability to lead the mind from the world of reality (appearance) to a contemplation of the divine order. The Abby Church at Cluny clearly demonstrates
the proof of the proportions of a church building as a classic musical ratio
function.

Figure 4.10.   Abbey Church Cluny, France.

The orientation of the monastery grounds, as was the church, were based on a formula laid down in both the rule and the liturgy. The church proper was on the north of the compound with the cloister on the south and the refractory farther south but at a right angle to the cloister walk. The Chapter house and rooms for novices were on the east of the compound with stairs leading to a second floor dormitory. The buildings at Cluny are constructed of pale stones with columns, pillars, and window but unlike St. Foy, there was no adornment. "We forbid there be any statues or pictures in our churches"[6] read their rule. The church was a regular rectangle with a series of square chapels attached that created a transept. And it, too, is a perfect 1:2 ratio. Within two centuries, though, things had changed drastically.

The Gothic style arose in France in the twelfth century and by its demise in the mid sixteenth century, had permeated Europe. Masonic guilds are most identified with this style which in itself demonstrates most clearly the religion of the Middle Ages. The great cathedrals of the age in France are located at St. Denis, Chartres, Bourges, and Notre Dame. In England they are located at Winchester, Salisbury, Lincoln, and Westminster. These magnificent structures demonstrated through a stratified approach, the richness of the design scheme as well as of the liturgy housed there. At the same time, these monuments indicate the rise of national consciousness with English architects like Elias de Dereham and Nicholas of Ely, the architect at Salisbury, creating an English as opposed to a French or German style. So too were the rituals and even church governance influenced by nationalism. Kings were "God's chosen" and with this authority appointed Bishops and Archbishops thus exercising a great deal of influence on the selection of the Pope as well as internal church governance. Rules of behavior for clergy and monks as well as instructions for religions architecture, and to a minor degree liturgy, had been a function of the secular court at least since the time of the Carolingian dynasty so this was nothing new. But with the urbanization of Europe much would change.

At Westminster, Henry III renovated the royal palace and had the magnificent abbey constructed in such a manner as to have the church and palace play prominent roles in the coronation or investiture ritual. The new abbey's ornate north entrance was sufficiently large to grant easy access to even the largest processions and flowed directly from the palace. The galleries which surrounded the transept were also large and elevated to enable spectators a full view of the event. And the crossing at the heart of the church was deliberately made massive to accommodate royal events. The church was also sufficiently lofty to accommodate knights on horse-back who rode under

Figure 4.11. Notre Dame, France.

Figure 4.12.   Westminster Abbey, England.

the congregation standing in the galleries and took their places, still mounted, in the wings of the transept.

As the Renaissance dawned in Europe and eventually reached England, changes in architectural style followed the awakening. The foundation of the new architectural style was provided by Leon Battista Alberti. The new Europe was the domain of merchants, bankers, and skilled craftsmen. The reawakening generated a new definition of human life. Scholars and artisans began to look to the past in order to recover strength for the future. A new life was breathed into the legacies of Rome and Greece. Sculptures were recovered, inscriptions deciphered, and these new humanists scoured the libraries of Europe seeking Classical wisdom. These antiquarian studies proved decisive and led to a movement away from Gothic design based on "arcane geometric formulae jealously guarded by the lodge"[7] which lacked specific proportion and had no fixed ratios, and in which a simple drawing or sketch provided the outline and design details were decided and executed on site through individual endeavor, to the development of a unitary plan created by a single architect. The ratios were simple and rational, based on classical learning. There were columns, pilasters, pediments, and niches. By the 1450s books on architecture such as Alberti's *Ten Books on Architecture*

Figure 4.13. Canterbury Cathedral, England.

based on Vitruvius, were being published. Function again became a fundamental aspect of design. New mathematical texts and the science of linear perspective make the secret knowledge of the craft lodges available to all. Buildings were created to demonstrate the structure of the natural world and nature was viewed as being synonymous with God.

In the lodges there was extreme unease. They were being replaced with "bookish" men who studied the past as well as mathematics, engineering, and natural philosophy. These new architects could not dress a stone nor turn a vault, but they were the precursors of a new age in which the craft guilds would have to reinvent themselves. Basic changes had come about in the rudimentary attitude about what made for good design and decorative frill alone no longer dominated European architecture. Brick began to replace stone by the end of the period with Henry VIII's great palace at Hampton Court, begun in 1515, being constructed from the cheaper, more available material. With this change in architecture went, as well, a change in ritual with the beginnings of the Reformation in Germany and in England, the creation of the first truly national church.

And just as church ritual expressed in liturgical drama moved from the nave to the steps and then to the plaza, so too did the urban master plan evolve away from the cathedral as its centerpiece to a more pageantry-focused style focused on the city itself. Cities no longer had rather random looks with narrow, winding lanes. New urban planning, especially in London after the great fire, saw the establishment of wide, straight streets with numerous plazas and public spaces. The function of architecture had now moved away from a setting for ritual alone toward a setting for public affairs similar to that utilized in Rome, much of which could be performed ritualistically. For the guilds, however, the essential element of ritual remained a core value in their communities and they took their principles with them into their lodges as governments assumed more of their operative functions.

A full understanding of the relationship between architecture and ritual requires us to understand that there are no truly archetypical forms. Romanesque, Gothic, Palladian, and Modern have their place and are worthy of

Figure 4.14.   Hampton Court, England.

study. So too the liturgies of Catholic and Protestant churches as well as other religious expression are worthy of analysis and scholarship. What are most worthy of study, though, are the human institutions and the identities of those people of all levels—kings and commoners—who created the structures that dot the country side and who daily engage in ritual. Both architecture and ritual are expressions of the human condition and directly impact on each other.

Masonic architecture follows the same symbolic, ritualistic pattern as that demonstrated in earlier religious architecture. The Lodge is described as a square within a square—a parallelepipedon--extending from east to west and north to south and, as were the great cathedrals, is symbolic of the world and of the Fraternity housed there indicating that both include all mankind. The Lodge is supported, metaphorically, by three great pillars which represent the principle tenets of wisdom, strength, and beauty. The Lodge, as a representation of the world, is covered by the starry heavens reached by a great ladder which demonstrates faith, hope, and charity. It is furnished first with an altar which symbolically may be assumed to represent the center of wisdom and it serves to support the Volume of Sacred Law as well as the significant symbols of Freemasonry--the Square and Compasses. The altar sits upon a pavement emblematical of the ground floor of the Temple of Solomon, the erection of which is the overriding allegory of Freemasonry. The pavement teaches us of the nature of human life, good and evil intertwined, and above is the blazing star which not only illuminates the Law, but also represents the Divinity.

Lodges, like early cathedrals, tend to have minimal or no illumination coming from without, depending, instead, on internal sources for light. Traditionally, Lodges had three great lights situated at the stations of the Worshipful Master, Senior Warden, and Junior Warden thus East, West, and South. There is no great light in the North and this is explained in terms of a representation of the original temple and its location relative to the meridian. Lodges are further furnished with a Rough and a Perfect Ashlar symbolizing the movement from imperfection to perfection. Lodges are dedicated in modern Freemasonry to St. John the Baptist and St. John the Evangelist, and within the room there is usually a definite representation of those Saints and their symbolic meaning to the Craft. Finally, each new Brother is instructed that Lodges are most often constructed on the second floor for security and also, possibly, in imitation of the architect's loft of the middle ages which was also traditionally on that floor. They are further told that each edifice is erected with the cornerstone placed in the northeast and so is each human Lodge symbolically so erected. The Entered Apprentice is, therefore, placed there to represent a sound beginning.

It is most instructive to compare the ritual and architecture of Freemasonry with that of the ritual practices of both in the convent and in the monastery. The attire of both the novice and the candidate are symbolic of a new set of values and a metaphor for a new beginning. The ritual requires not only utilization of a clearly defined space, but also physical control of the body is demanded which serves as a metaphor for that life that has been chosen. The candidate's movements in the degrees, as are the novice's in the investiture, include circumambulation which represents a movement of one's own free will and accord in front of the company or congregation to symbolize the beginning of a journey. Both the novice and the candidate walk barefoot to the altar—sacred ground—though Freemasonry has somewhat modified this practice to meet the allusion to a pledge of sincerity and divesture as found in the Book of Ruth. Novices prostrate themselves before the altar while candidates kneel there. And, at the proper time, both are invested with the clothing and marks of their new station. The candidate has forsaken the profane as the novice has forsaken the real world. It is a new beginning for both.

It is also worthy of consideration while instructing initiates, to give them a fuller understanding of the mysteries of ritual architecture. In our Fellow Craft lecture the Brother is informed that a point establishes a line which can define a plane and then a solid. Simple instruction in basic geometric principles may help clarify this lecture. Demonstrating how two pins (points) and a piece of string may be used to establish a line and, in turn, divide that line proportionally is an interesting exercise in the mysteries of the early craft guild. Add to this the utilization of those same simple items—pins and string—and a demonstration can be done to show how to create a perfect ninety-degree angle and, in turn, a perfect square or rectangle as in the Masonic square within a square. One last demonstration using the same simple tools helps the new Brother visualize the mystery of orienting a structure due east and west without a magnetic compass or modern transit.

Further demonstrations of the mysteries of operative masonry may include the construction of a perfect spiral stair case along with an explanation of why the stairs curve to the right or left when entered from top or bottom. Going a step further, a demonstration of the utilization of a square to create a transept vault, the fundamental feature of medieval cathedrals, is impressive and instructional, again in terms of explaining mysteries and secrets. On the structural side, an explanation of vault construction or the rounded arch with a drawing of the support structure may be used to demonstrate the need for sound instruction and the responsibility of the Master in the process (the master removed the final support in the framework, if the arch collapsed, he would pay the price). It is also sometimes of interest to initiates to view the progress of the mason's arts and their mysteries through a review of the progress of the simple arch from the barrel with its dependence upon the keystone to the loftier Gothic and on to the Ogee.

On a more mysterious level, initiates often find explanations of reflection and refraction of interest, especially in terms of how they are used in reality and symbolically to express focus. Properly ground or cast window rosettes, for example, can focus sunlight on the altar to emphasize ritual and liturgy. This may be accompanied with a brief description of the physics of light, again as employed by utilizing ground glass pieces colored red, green, and blue, to create a perfectly white light within the cathedral to surround the high altar. Finally, even modern fiction, properly vetted, may be used to demonstrate ancient techniques as well as the movement of architectural principles from Italy to northern Europe during the Renaissance. Ken Follett's *World Without End* gives a fair depiction of an architect's loft as well as suggesting the rediscovery of architectural principles in Italy and their migration throughout Europe.

The intent of such instruction is to bring life to what might otherwise be seen by some as a relatively dry, arcane subject and to make sure that all Brothers know that they have become part of an ancient tradition based soundly in education and proper performance of the work. There were truly masonic secrets, but they were trade secrets usually associated with recognition and proficiency, and are thus no more mysterious than how to create a right angle. But to the initiated in the Middle Ages, these secrets insured employment and, through the guild system, they indemnified the structure and thus the reputation of the craft. It is no different in the modern era; a thorough understanding of Masonic mysteries insures the continued existence and strength of the Craft.

NOTES

1. Nadia Drake. "Neanderthals Built Mysterious Stone Circles," in *National Geographic,* May, 2016, located at http://news.nationalgeographic.com/2016/05/neanderthals-caves-rings-building-archeology.

2. Klaus Schmidt. "Gobekli Tepe, Southeastern Turkey: A Preliminary Report on the 1995-1999 Excavations." *Paleorient 26, No. 1,* 2001, 46.

3. Kostof, Spiro. *A History of Architecture: Settings and Ritual Second Edition.* (New York: Oxford University Press, 1995), 19.

4. Alberge, Dalya. "Stonehenge may have been first erected in Wales, evidence suggests." Located at http://www.theguardian.com/uk-news/2015/dec/07/stonehenge-first-erected-in-wales. Retrieved, December 21, 2015.

5. Kostof, *A History of Architecture,* 324.

6. Kostof, *A History of Architecture,* 324.

7. Kostof, *A History of Architecture,* 405.

Chapter Five

Ritual and Theatre

The roots of theatre are social drama; images of past experiences elicit feelings which produce meaning. Ritual like theatre is a structured experience.

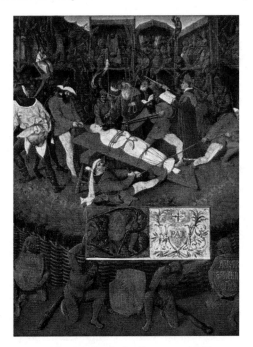

Figure 5.1.   Martyrdom of St. Apollonia by Fouquet, 1445.

Masonic ritual is often described as a set of allegorical plays whose purpose is to propound the Fraternity's philosophy which is friendship, morality, and brotherly love. The Craft in its own ritual refers to itself as a "beautiful

67

system of morality, veiled in allegory and illustrated by symbols," or as "a beautiful and peculiar system of morality." Common to all modern Freemasonry is a three-degree system based on an allegorical recounting of the construction of King Solomon's Temple in Jerusalem. The degree work or ritual is scripted and all movements are described in detail in various cyphered manuals. The work is done from memory and, while there is some commonality from jurisdiction to jurisdiction, each jurisdiction or Grand Lodge tends to adjust or standardize its ritual based upon its perception of Masonic tradition as well as the history of the origins of that particular Grand Lodge. Some Grand Lodges in the United States do not have an adopted ritual with each constituent Lodge permitted to use the ritual they desire. In other Grand Lodges, such as the Grand Lodge of Kentucky, there are several rituals that Lodges use at their discretion.

Symbolic or Blue Lodge Freemasonry made its appearance in the Colonies in 1730, about thirteen years after its founding in London. Its degrees were originally rather simple though they evolved after about 1750 into a structure recognizable in the modern world. The Scottish Rite of Freemasonry came into being in the United States with the formation of the Mother Supreme Council in Charleston, South Caroline, in May 1801. Its founders were known as the "Eleven Gentlemen of Charleston." In terms of degree work and ritual, the Scottish Rite, even more than the Symbolic Lodge, utilizes one-act plays staged in costume with appropriate lighting, effects, and scenery to examine the different philosophies, religions, and ethical systems propounded in each degree. The intent of these plays is not to tell a Brother what to think, but rather to make available to them examples useful for self-reflection and examination. A similar format is followed in the various York Rite Degrees. At the Symbolic Lodge, the core of modern Freemasonry, the dramatic nature of degree work is most recognizable in the last degree with the first two being primarily instructive.

Freemasonry arose in the late sixteenth and early seventeenth centuries in England and other European countries. The first records of what would become modern Freemasonry come from Edinburgh Lodge No. 1 and are dated 1599. Elias Ashmole in his diary for 16 October 1646 notes that on that day he was "made a Free-Mason." The minutes of Edinburgh Lodge at Mary's Chapel for July 1634 note that Lord Alexander and his brother were made Masons and in 1686 Dr. Robert Plott wrote in his *Natural History of Staffordshire* that it was the custom "especially in Staffordshire" to admit men into the Society of Freemasons. A more complete account of the early ritual-- Making a Mason—may be found in Chapter I. Based on the comments made by Ashmole and Plott as well as those found in the various early minutes, the process was markedly simple. It was never-the-less, ritual and theatrical in presentation and format.

Ritual is a staged event that provides a means for transformation in those involved. Theatre is also staged and, in its original format, was intended to result in change or catharsis from the Greek word κάθαρσις meaning "purification" or "cleansing" through art. The word is used as a metaphor by Aristotle in the *Poetics,* in noting the effects of tragedy—the first type of drama--on the mind of the spectator. The term may also apply to comedy but at no point does Aristotle explain the meaning of the word. D. W. Lucas in his book on the *Poetics* refers to catharsis as being devoted to pity, fear, purification, and intellectual clarification. Modern literary critics and theorists tend to view catharsis strictly as providing to the audience intellectual clarification with some accompanying emotional impact.

Community life is at the center of both ritual and theatre. And as humanity has advanced intellectually so too has it advanced in its use and manipulation of symbols or symbolic communication. We have become accustomed to devising acceptable cultural methods for dealing with crisis and establishing modes of redress symbolically rather than physically. The world has now become a place of values, significance, and meaning, a "world of the mind" which is expressed through ritual. Complex and often obscure philosophical and ethical problems are addressed in both theatre and ritual thus enabling the community to survive and to pass to future generations its values and mores. "Meaning" is assigned to events and an imaginative understanding is made possible. The "performance" has nothing to do with "form" but rather, based upon its origins in the Old French *parfourni,* means that the action has been thoroughly carried out. An experience is intensified by ritualized performance; the past has been evoked and dealt with; feelings are addressed; and meaning is established. The full experience comes only, though, when it has been expressed and has become intelligible to others. Ritual could well be described, as is theatre, as a "structured unit of experience."[1]

Ritual tends to denote a perilous passage performed for the good of the community. It is, effectively, a "passing through" which, like any ferry ride, requires a fare. It is "experience" (which means "to try or test") and through experience's "fearful perils" the candidate willingly moves forward learning through his actions.

Early theatre in Britain sprang from liturgical enactments or performances which had strong roots in the cathedrals, convents, and monasteries of medieval England. As early as the tenth century, liturgical dramas had emerged in Germany inspired by the classical works of Terrance. And while scholars disagree on whether the extant texts were ever staged, the nature of the notes suggests that they were. The oldest such drama is *Dulcitius* which tells the story of three noble-ranking Christian sisters imprisoned by Diocletian for refusing to renounce their faith (similar to the Legend of the Four Crowned Martyrs of Masonic tradition which names the same Roman emperor). The oldest two sisters are burnt while the younger, enslaved to a brothel, is sacrificed on a mountain top. The play demonstrates the triumph of the new over the old and includes dramatic events—death and sacrifice—accompanied by miraculous happenings. It establishes a clear distinction between the old way of doing things and the new. This is exactly what happens in Masonic ritual.

Many people considered it curious if not impossible to accept that drama developed in the sanctuary, the center of the religious world. But the sanctuary is meant to illustrate life and the rituals performed there are teaching tools which provide instructions on a variety of subjects not just ethics and morals. Ritual in this form also serves to address the issue of unregulated practices thus resulting in an extension of the community as a governing agent over space and time. As noted in the chapter on architecture, the space utilized in ritual was representative of culture of the time and reflected a specific understanding of the world as well as of social identify. Some spaces were better guarded than others, and some entirely forbidden to the profane or uninitiated. Ritual, as does drama, also suggests that it is not necessary that one participate first-hand in the events or locations described. Enclosure does not necessarily imply lack of exposure. The men who wrote Masonic ritual clearly demonstrate that they had a firm foundation in the external world as found in classical literature, scholarship, and, above all, a profound, in-depth understanding of Scripture.

As liturgical ritual expanded and became more expressive as well as more dramatic, it required additional space and personnel. And expansion led it to changed or morphed into something else. While there is no clear evidence that church liturgy lead directly to the mystery plays which first became popular in continental Europe in the twelfth century and remained popular in England until the sixteenth century, there is no doubt that various forms of dramatic reenactment of religiously themed events had become common by the late medieval period. At issue in the understanding of this movement is the fact that the majority of church records and texts were destroyed during the Reformation in England and most of those which survived, met their demise during the Commonwealth.

As noted also in the chapter on architecture, much of church drama and ritual were directly related to church services which were framed by the building itself. The altar was the focal point and the relationship between interior spaces reflected upon the narrative. The Mass itself was a dramatic allegory as well as a remembrance. John Gassner suggests that processions within the church reflect the physical structure of the building defining the structure as a religious space. Early churches had no fixed pews and were thus essentially large rectangular open spaces with congregants often standing against the walls. The structure and the ritual suggest that the parishioners are being watched by an invisible God and that both the space and the performance reflected His divine order. The very ground plan of the medieval church with its transept is, suggests David Wiles, a perfect replica of the human body and thus at the focal point of all ritual action with the heart at the center. And the rituals which involved sprinkling, touching, or laying on of hands as well as signs, kneeling, and the like enabled the acts to imprint upon the mind the customs of the culture and the meaning of the liturgy.

In both theatre and ritual, participants and spectators create meaning as they perform and witness. In this mode, ritual serves as an affective meditation with the area utilized serving to define time, space, and history for the event. Fraternities are no different. Early confraternities or religious fraternities named themselves after saints, religious feasts, urban locations, or craft guild patrons (Four Crowned Martyrs for masons) and established spaces by assuming the responsibility for the upkeep of chapels and altars dedicated to those saints. As craft guilds developed in the middle ages, they assumed this responsibility as well as the staging of mystery and morality plays, especially those directly related to their trade. These early liturgical and dramatic spaces were then adapted to the Lodge and, in turn, shaped the lives of the participants.

In the late medieval period, the mystery plays, especially in England, became major festivals that displayed both guild and civic power. They were able to straddle the secular and the sacred worlds, and combined celebrations which were dynamic yet met the demands of changing circumstances. They demonstrated how the sacred and the secular worlds mixed as does Masonic ritual. As these religiously-focused entertainments (mystery and morality plays) met their demise, the very identity of the producing fraternities and guild came into question. For example, when the St. George Fraternity, formed to produce the St. George Play, reframed itself into the Company and Citizens of Saint George it surrendered its religious affiliation even though it continued to hold banquets, perform plays, and initiate members well into the reign of Edward VI. Guild rituals proved malleable and their activities moved from a religious to a civic focus. By the late 1500s, this evolution witnessed the guilds alter their activities to become even more civic and, for the St. George Fraternity, they moved their main celebrations to dates that coincided with civic events such as the installation of the city mayor in Norwich thus migrating from a religious to a civic focus. The movement from emplacement (within the church proper) to displacement (without the church proper even to the point of civic only engagements) allowed the fraternity to reintegrate its celebrations into the social fabric. The Guild of Masons (or Freemasons) followed much the same path: from liturgical to civic and fraternal.

The development of urban centers and civic spirit that began in the thirteenth century came in unison with the establishment of both civic identity and trade and craft guilds. All urban centers depended upon developing and maintaining trade as well as upon various organizational structures. Cities were deemed well-regulated when their guilds flourished and their fairs and trading centers attracted visitors. Visitors served to enhance mercantile reputation and provided the city's elite with sense of pride. The visitor, like the visitor to the cathedral, viewed the architecture as a semiotic code. The massive walls symbolized strength and protection, while the formal structures within the walls such as the church and the plaza symbolized power and wealth. So, too, did the plays demonstrate craft identify, mastery, wealth, and influence. And as the mystery and morality plays moved from church yard to city streets as they did at York and Chester, the guilds assumed virtually full control. These plays provided not only civic identity; they also enabled the guilds to demonstrate their craft and their organizational skills as well as their commitment to their community.

Essential to these plays which were formatted as a processional was a sense of pilgrimage to a sacred or dedicated space. The route, as it is in Masonic ritual, was a "difficult ground", a symbolic "rough and rugged road" for the participants that was arranged in such a manner as to benefit the audience—the partakers of ritual. The performances were carefully aligned to enhance the meaning of the event and to create a proper picture of order and unity through the appearances, actions, and words of those participating. Ritual routes were not, however, straight lines and often involved circumambulation with the cathedral, town hall, and, above all, the guild hall prominently displayed. These medieval ritual performances provided the audience with the opportunity to construct a narrative. Each audience member and each participant interpreted the event in terms of their own perceptions, knowledge of the story, and their relationship with other spectators.

Generally, the citizens (guild members and others) were responsible for all technical elements of the performance, but civic dignitaries tended to become the center of focus. Yet, these ritualistic performances provided the opportunity for social differentiations to be diminished and the wholeness of the community demonstrated. The ordinary citizen is both spectator and participant, and unlike the cloistered rituals of earlier centuries, membership became more expansive. Homogeneity is achieved as the participants surrender their individuality for the good of the community. The value of such ritual comes from its ability to free participants to search out and discover meaning in ways that transcend traditional communication. The performers were both actively and passively involved as were the spectators. It is exactly the same in Masonic ritual with the performers and those on the sidelines becoming involved in the dynamic actions described.

The St. Thomas pageant performed at Canterbury in the early sixteenth century to depict the martyrdom of Thomas a Becket displays some striking similarities with Masonic ritual of the present day. Becket is struck down by four knights who formed a conspiracy and his violent death is later memorialized when his remains are returned to Canterbury and interred in a well-marked shrine. The feasts of St. Thomas were celebrated on 29 December—the date of his death—and on 7 July to mark his elevation to sainthood. The pageant of his martyrdom was typically performed in early July and reflects the first intersection between religious and civic drama. The order of march for the ritual was laid down in a hierarchical manner with city fathers followed by constables and sheriffs. By 1537 the religious nature of the procession was being played down and by the end of the reign of Henry VIII the pageant had been suppressed to disappear completely under the reign of Edward VI. What is most interesting about the St. Thomas pageant, according to the records maintained by the court of Elizabeth I, is that one Mr. Ardem bought the cart used to present the pageant and took it to "the guildhall." Which guildhall is not specified in the records, though.

One of the most prominent medieval guilds was that of the Mercers. They staged "The Last Judgement" in the York Mystery Cycle. The cycle involved forty-eight plays sponsored predominately by the various guilds and was performed at Midsummer close to St. Johns Day. The Mercers were the richest and most powerful guild of their time and thus responsible for the most dramatic and elaborate of the plays— "The Last Judgement." The presentation utilized symbolic decorative angels to represent heaven with other symbols including clouds and rainbows, as well as representations of heaven and hell to symbolically demonstrate God's covenant with the people. The display included painted canvases and floor cloths with the viewing space tightly regulated to facilitate a more dramatic presentation.

It is evident, then, that theatrical presentations were not simply expelled from the church and from religious life. Religious organizations and churches remained at the focal point of such activity. What happened is that the presentations evolved as spectatorship increased; as wealth and urbanity enabled more elaborate presentations; as civic and guild sponsorship and involvement increased; and as the action became less theological and more allegorical. The Shipbuilders who produced the Noah play at York and the Skinners whose wears were displayed in the "Entry into Jerusalem" viewed the new pageants as useful advertising which enabled the audience to become emotionally involved with the characters which exercising critical judgement about the goods displayed and the technical proficiency demonstrated. At York the cycle plays depicted labor in the vineyards describing craftsmen as seeking recognition for the perfection of their labor thus reflecting upon the guilds' stress on quality of workmanship and excellence of labor. This was appropriate subject matter which both city and guild used to justify their activities. Plays eight and nine in the York Cycle are of interest to Freemasons because they involved the building of Noah's Ark and the story of the flood. The theme of labor is explored in the Noah plays at both York and Chester with the guild at Chester displaying its prowess in the use of axe, hatchet, and hammer.

The overriding metaphor of all medieval cycles is that of a journey that is essential to life. This journey begins with birth, progresses through childhood to maturity, and moves on to the inevitable adventure of death. It is the journey from earth to heaven. And like the Grail legend, the Legend of Noah, the Hiramic Legend, and other epic stories, quests, pilgrimages, and trials cause man to reassess and prevail. By the late sixteenth and early seventeenth centuries, these dramatic productions not only shrunk in size and importance, they also moved indoors and to become the domain of the Guildhall, the Inns of Court, and the royal palace. But what happened indoors was little different from what had been seen on the church step or the city plaza except in size.

Typically, the pageants were presented in inns which may also have provided an upper room for a guild or fraternity. The room became the centerpiece and was often decorated symbolically to represent some other place such as the Temple of Solomon. The audience tended to sit on either side of the main hall (see Chapter IV on architecture) and, because the space was indoors, the acoustics were greatly improved as was the comfort factor of the spectators who could now sit rather than stand. These indoor performances also became more polished and could be produced on a more regular schedule without regard to weather. Decorum, as well, came into focus with a new understanding of manners prevalent. Outward displays of etiquette became important and the head of the house or guild became the ritual leader with the guests and servants providing the supporting characters. During this period also, English society became relatively mobile and travel (traveling man) became an accepted part of life. This forged links between communities and served to bind England into a nation.

A popular theme of the inside dramas was temptation. Man is tempted by sin, avarice, greed, or mischief to plot against his fellows and to sin. Moral correctness is explored and the relationship between such morality and earthly labor addressed. The major themes were established clearly at the beginning of the mini-dramas, as they are in the Second Section of the Master Mason Degree. Topical issues are usually raised and vices displayed. The spectators were carefully drawn into the moral action with the audience being both witness and, often, jury. In the indoor dramas few costumes were used and prop pieces rather than scenery predominated. The devices used were more symbolic that realistic.

Medieval theatre and ritual varied as widely as does modern Masonic performance and ritual. The purpose then was as it is now, to attract an audience and to focus its attention on the actions and the moral decisions displayed. In their earliest years, the audience was more actively involved and often addressed directly at the beginning of the play, but as time passed, direct audience participation dwindled. The problem with interpreting early drama as well as early ritual is that of frame of reference. The "Play of the Sacraments" performed at Croxton serves as an example. Modern audiences perceive it as anti-Semitic, but it should be viewed instead as an indication of prevailing thinking and anxieties. To understand fully the meaning of ritual and allegory, it is necessary to come to grips with the time in which the original presentation was made and the prevailing social, legal, and religious thought of that age. The punishments meted out to the ruffians in the Hiramic Legend appear exceedingly harsh to a modern audience. For the early eighteenth century British citizen, however, they were not harsh and, as are the penalties spoken of in all three degrees, reflected British military and civil law.

Early religious drama and liturgical ritual are close cousins and their relationship with their audiences were well understood in their day. The morals taught had meaning for the audience and the experiences described were common to all. They were little different in intent and impact than what we expect to be accomplished through modern Masonic ritual.

NOTE

1. Victor Turner. *From Ritual to Theatre: The Human Seriousness of Play.* (New York: PAJ Publications), 198 p. 15.

Chapter Six

Esotericism in Ritual

When we consider a book, we mustn't ask ourselves what it says but what it means,
a precept that the commentators on the holy books
very clearly had in mind.
—Umberto Eco in *The Name of the Rose*

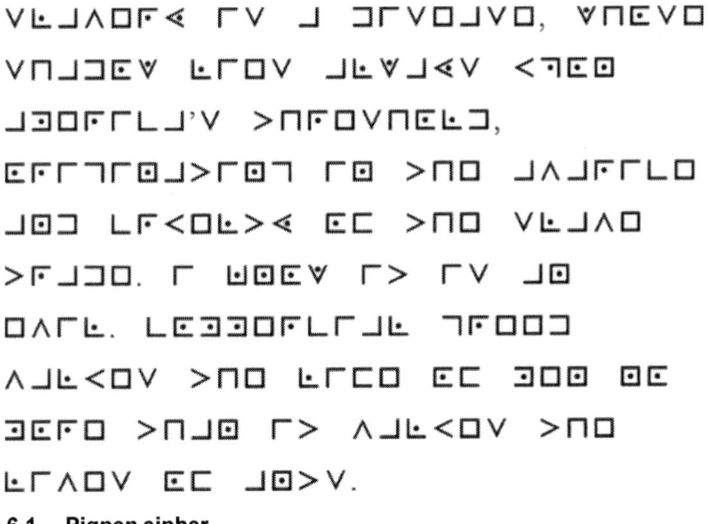

VᘈJΛ�□F⋖ ⌐V J ⊐⌐V□JV□, ∀⊓ᘰV□
V⊓JƆᘰ∀ ᘈ⌐□V Jᘈ∀J⋖V ⋖⊓ᘰ□
JƆ□⌐⌐LJ'V >⊓F□V⊓ᘰᘈƆ,
ᘰ⌐⌐⊓⌐□J>⌐□⊓ ⌐□ >⊓□ JΛJF⌐L□
J□Ɔ L⌐⋖□ᘈ>⋖ ᘰᘈ >⊓□ VᘈJΛ□
>⌐JƆ□. ⌐ ᗺ□ᘰ∀ ⌐> ⌐V J□
□Λ⌐ᘈ. Lᘰ⊐Ɔ□⌐L⌐Jᘈ ⌐F□□Ɔ
ΛJᘈ⋖□V >⊓□ ᘈ⌐�ᘰ□ ᘰᘈ ⊐□□ □ᘰ
ƆᘰF□ >⊓J□ ⌐> ΛJᘈ⋖□V >⊓□
ᘈ⌐Λ□V ᘰᘈ J□>V.

Figure 6.1. Pigpen cipher.

Masonic ritual is strongly based in the Western philosophical esoteric tradition and the societies which utilized it which permeated Europe beginning in the sixteenth century and found their expression in the United States beginning in the eighteenth century. The symbols of the square, compasses, plumb, level, star, columns, and rose, coupled in the eighteenth and nineteenth centuries with a renewed interested in astrology, enabled special forms of thought to be transmitted throughout a community. Symbols and reality were placed into a concordism which displayed Nature's harmony and aided in the acquisition of knowledge about each. The cosmos was perceived as a complex and multilayered structure in which "light" or some type of "hidden" knowledge, often described as fire, was obtainable through contemplation. To know the world and man's place in it—a sense of *gnosis*—led to a meditative world filled with symbolic representations of the triad of God, Humanity, and Nature.

Esotericism provides for the development and expansion of serendipitous thinking which enables the individual to imagine and meditate. The imagination facilitates the development of symbols and images into a fuller understanding of spiritual mysteries. It is a tool for knowledge of the world, the self, and the myth or legend. It reveals significations and serves to enlarge our world view. Visionary imagination as a philosophy took full form at the beginning of the seventeenth century concurrent with the rise of Freemasonry in Europe and was influenced directly by both Jewish and Christian esoteric traditions.

The esoteric tradition has traditionally embraced the concept of transmutation as an essential component. This aspect of the tradition is often misinterpreted to mean the physical change of a base element into a precious one. The true importance of esotericism as well as of initiation rituals, however, is representative of a transformation or passage from one place to another or one status to another, and not of one substance to another. A metamorphosis takes place through esoteric ritual which represents a renewal, a second chance, another opportunity, or a reaffirmation. It may also be viewed as an attempt to recover something that has been lost. A new path is taken and an old one is discarded. This mystical tradition includes purgation (divestment), illumination, and unification. This archetypical approach to tradition is most marked in "modern" times beginning in the late fifteenth century with the Renaissance and extended into the Enlightenment as well as into the modern world. It led to new academic explorations and influenced the study of comparative religion. It is soundly based in the concept that there is an overarching truth found in all religious and esoteric traditions. And this truth may be taught or transmitted because the knowledge is valid and the initiation is a master to disciple process. A person cannot initiate himself, the mysteries are passed, not created piecemeal.

The esoteric tradition of transmutation is often paralleled with that of the medieval alchemist in that something of a lesser value is to be transformed into something of a higher value. Jungian psychology would view this as the movement from the state of being will-less to that of being self-actualized. Maslow may have interpreted it as the movement through his hierarchy. Philosophically, this process is related directly to man becoming more in tune with his God through correct moral action and a sound system of moral instruction. The forms of symbolism used in this tradition are well known; it is the esoteric interoperation that proves difficult to understand.

In esotericism, *mythos* and *logos* meet. The myth or legend is to be contemplated and explored for its meaning with the natural relationship between God, man, and the universe being explained. The narrative, rich with symbols but not to be accepted as literal fact, expresses the splendor of the work and human life therein finds its meaning. English Freemasonry and its derivative as practiced in the United States is less esoteric than other mystery traditions yet both maintain a strong sense of symbolism and esoteric communication. The higher degrees in Freemasonry, especially those found in the Scottish Rite (or in the United Kingdom, the Rose Croix) which are not of English origin, are the most esoteric. The thirty-three degrees of the Scottish Rite build on the moral and philosophical teachings of Symbolic Lodge Freemasonry. They appear to have originated at some point prior to 1733 and there is a specific reference in the Copiale cipher of the mid-1730s to "the rank of a Scottish master" as being an "entirely new invention."[1] The other large appendant Masonic body is the York Rite which includes Royal Arch Masons, Council of Royal and Select Masters or Cryptic Masons, and the Commandery of the Knights Templar. This separate body operates with some autonomy and is based on the Legend of York. Three of the degrees in this body are based on what was perceived as the Templar Code and is open only to Christian Masons. Within Symbolic Lodge Freemasonry, there appears to have been a movement referred to by some as Strict Observance based on the Templar Code, but, by the beginning of the nineteenth century, many Symbolic Lodge Freemasons had abandoned the flirtation with the Templars and moved toward the more universal acceptance Fraternity common in the modern world.

As the world moved into the eighteenth century and Western Christian philosophy dominated critical thinking, Masonic ceremonies and rituals emphasized even more the acquisition of knowledge (light) and a legitimate transformation within the individual. Serious reflection was undertaken on the great monotheisms of Judaism, Christianity, and Islam, and links between the three were explored and elaborated upon. The theological and philosophical as well as dramatic writings of Gotthold Ephraim Lessing serve to illuminate this movement. And while the landscape became filled with allusions and direct references to the occult, and both publishing and, in the twentieth century, electronic media, were filled with supposed metaphysical, religious, and fraternal mysteries more commonly and sensationally called "secrets," the sound esoteric tradition of past generations prevailed among the more enlightened and dedicated members of the Craft.

The twentieth century Western esoteric tradition grew further by embracing scholarly historians of the phenomenon. Historians, both specialists and generalists, began to research, write, and publish their findings and conclusions. They sought to give status to their discipline and gain a more public understanding of their much maligned field. Freemasons were often confronted with the historical charge that their "speculative" nature as expressed in constitutions published after 1717 tended to separate them from the traditional initiatory and symbolic esoteric world with its firm foundation in a belief in Deity. This is, in fact, untrue and, as demonstrated in the first constitutions and all that followed, there is in the Fraternity an inseparable relationship between God and man. The Deity provides the light, not man. And though several Christian churches, notably Catholicism, some Pentecostal groups, and, even, some more main-line denominations, have expressed the belief that esoteric Freemasonry is not compatible with Christian faith, this represents a gross misunderstanding of the Fraternity's principles and is possibly based on some Christian theologians objecting to the link between faith and knowledge thus expressing the unjustified concern that the Masonic quest for "light" in some way interferes with a pure expression of faith. Knowledge seeks to question, explain, and grasp reality fully—internal and external. Knowledge is what Einstein would call the soup, not the flavor. It is that which enables us to rediscover the relationship between man and his Creator.

Esotericism is a form of indirect communication which utilizes symbols and is neither unorthodox nor relegated to any period, century, civilization, or organization. "The world," says Sherlock Holmes in *The Hound of the Baskervilles,* "is full of obvious things which nobody by any chance ever observes." Ancient philosophers tended to embrace double doctrines: external or exoteric and internal or esoteric; one profane, the other mysterious. Esoteric knowledge was considered appropriate only for thoughtful seekers of knowledge and truth. Esoteric writing preserved this special brand of knowledge for a hand-picked audience which had "wits of such sharpness as can pierce the veil."[2] It was an internal restraint expressed externally created to avoid political and religious persecution for, as Thomas Aquinas noted in 1258, "certain things can be explained in private which we should keep silent about in public."[3] Maimonides echoes Aquinas a century later writing that "these matters [theology] are only for a few solidary individuals of a very special sort."[4] In the tenth-century Abu Nasor al-Farabi wrote of Plato that "he followed the practice of using symbols, riddles, obscurity, and difficulty, so that science would not fall into the hands of those who do not deserve it and are deformed, or into the hands of one who does not know its worth or who use it improperly."[5]

Modern Freemasonry is an intensely complex and contradictory phenomenon which has meant different things at different times in different places and been thus practiced. Its members have included numerous serious thinkers, scientists, politicians, academics, and public leaders who used the Fraternity's principles and teachings to advance progressive ideas and to counterpoise civil, religious, and academic institutions. Masonic Lodges served the spread of enlightened thinking in a much more theologically conservative age and facilitated the development of social order out of the chaos that plagued Europe from the sixteenth through the late eighteenth centuries. And when it came to the New World, especially that portion which would become the United States, a number of that nation's founders joined the Fraternity and, according to Reinhart Koselleck, there were two social structures which left a "decisive imprint" on the Age of Enlightenment, "the Republic of Letters and the Masonic Lodge."[6] Esoteric writing and the practice of transmitting knowledge through esoteric means was formalized in these Lodges and resulted in an expansion of the Enlightenment through the vast literature associated with the organization which made common use of pseudonyms and anonymity to explain, illustrate, and shed light upon the character of this "new" philosophy while protecting the authors from public and political retribution. The very creation of modern open society required those changes both in Europe and North America, and their success depended upon esoteric secrecy.

Esoteric writing is found in four forms: defensive, protective, pedagogical, and political. Defensive esotericism refers to philosophical writings that shield the author from some harm (persecution) while protective esotericism focuses on shielding society from "perilous" truths. The protective form of esotericism comes closest to describing the Masonic motivation to protect its mysteries. Political esotericism is intended to result in political, civil, or religious change or reform while protecting the author and limiting the information to those capable of understanding while pedagogical esotericism focuses on philosophical education of the rare and gifted in our society. Of the four types of esoteric writing, the protective form is considered the most profound and as such meets the most resistance. It is based on the assumption that some truths may be harmful or dangerous in the hands of the uninitiated. "A little bit of knowledge is a dangerous thing" goes the old adage. Ancient writers recounted numerous stories which enabled the reader to reflect upon how humans have reacted when they came into possession of information they were not prepared to handle or worthy of possessing: they had not been initiated and instructed. The Tree of Knowledge, the Tower of Babel, the myth of Prometheus, and the Sirens encountered by Odysseus demonstrate the perils of esoteric knowledge when confronted by the uninitiated. The same admonition is found in Plato's *Republic* and the Ernst and Faulk dialogues of Lessing which dramatize the hazards of the acquisition by the unprepared of certain forms of knowledge. Truth does not always turn out to match our hopes and dreams, the esoteric writers warn, nor does reality always conform to the demands of the human heart or soul. Seeing the truth, suggests philosophers, is often exalted above the capacity of the common man and requires special initiation and instruction.

The Jewish Kabbalistic tradition is solidly esoteric and prides itself in that form of expression. It is open about its secretiveness and is based soundly upon the common assumption that some knowledge may confuse some people. The Talmud, the second most important set of Jewish writings, requires that certain information not be "expounded" before other than "a Sage," and Maimonides writes that ancient sages "enjoined us to discuss these subjects privately . . . and then only if he be wise and capable of independent reasoning," finishing the paragraph by stating that "it is left to him to develop the conclusions for himself and to penetrate the depths of that subject."[7]

Christianity has a similar discipline of the secret or tradition of protective esotericism. The Catholic *Encyclopedia* devotes an entire entry to the subject. The tradition is founded in the parables and words of Jesus who, in Matthew 13:10-17, states that he would speak plainly to them (the disciples) but in parables to others, and Aquinas, commenting on Boethius, supports Paul's comment in I Corinthians 3: 1-2 that he could not give them the highest wisdom concerning God because it is only for the truly transcendent man to understand. Aquinas then states that "certain things can be explained to the wise in private which we should keep silent about in public."[8] Natural science and natural philosophy, both profane and divine, as well as Freemasonry are cloaked in riddles and parables.

Freemasonry has experienced a prolonged development both in doctrine and ritual, but only recently have Masonic scholars as well as other academics become interested in those initiatory societies which utilize esotericism to transmit information and mysteries. Western esotericism has been transmitted traditionally through rituals of initiation which demonstrate the totality of ancient religious practices. The candidate is being transformed from an old to a new state. The mystery transmitted esoterically contains knowledge that is intended to transmute the candidate at an internal level into a new person. The candidate is generally passive and humble in manner, being led through the ceremony by a conductor and obeying their orders. The candidate is often instructed to fear no danger and place his blind trust in the society and his guide. These initiation rituals are intended to develop intense fellowship or comradeship as well as trust and egalitarianism or equality. They are common to military, civic, religious, and fraternal organizations.

Freemasonry is not, as so commonly described by media, a secret society but rather it is a society with secrets generally associated with methods of recognition; with rituals that have been developed over centuries; and with a philosophy that utilizes esoteric knowledge and transmission techniques. By treating secrecy and mystery ritually, the Fraternity moves them from the ordinary and imparts upon its mysteries and rituals a spiritual dimension. The esoteric veil constitutes part of the message. Rituals and symbols have always had multiple meanings—primary or immediate ones, and allusive or hidden ones. The awareness that the veil constitutes part of the message is considered of utmost importance by most Masonic ritualist. And though truly esoteric rituals do not appear to have entered the world of Freemasonry until the mid-eighteenth century through the higher degrees, the extant evidence indicates that early craft masonry was moral in character with ritualistic procedures used to initiate and instruct new workmen. By the 1650s, however, solid links began to emerge linking ritual, esotericism, and Freemasonry.

The meanings of symbols for humans are often elusive, vague, and convoluted, but meaning is capable of discovery and understanding through research, investigation, and explanation. And just as language is constituted of units—phonemes, morphemes, and words—so too is esoteric ritual constituted of discrete symbolic acts. But the meaning of the symbols and the ritual are grasped only through cultural transformation or initiation. Yet while ritual may appear to exalt the outward or the contrived, when fully understood, it becomes an inward expression of an external reality. Thus esotericism has served its purpose. Only the select ones have received the preserved knowledge and are thus capable of passing it, unimpaired, to future generations of initiates.

Humans are cultural animals and prefer to live in societies. From the beginning of society there has been a communal conception of the right way to live as well as a shared view of morality and the sacred. The basic concept was that we needed to join together. People are, Aquinas wrote in *City of God*, "bound together by a common agreement as to the objects of their love."[9] The flaw in human reasoning, though, is that while the lowest levels of life described in Maslow's "Hierarchy of Needs" as physiological and safety (air, water, food, personal security, and health) are self-evident; higher requirements such as love, esteem, and self-actualization, because they are mentally elevated and internal, are less clear and less understood. At these upper levels there is a weakened sense of certainty and stability, a condition feared by many. In the modern world, communities or societies of common interest serve to ameliorate that concern by bringing into harmony through philosophic interchange questions about higher certainties. And while authority is often rooted in tradition and custom, reason and custom may also provide guidance for human thought and action.

Humans are complex entities with a variety of illusions, beliefs, perceptions, questions, faculties, and desires. Most of the questions humans have about life and the world are practical and not of an academic nature. They do not require an abstract or complex answer. Instinct, habit, custom, laws, traditions, and mores generally suffice to address most of our issues. But a crucial element of human interaction is our moral commitment to each other's welfare as well as that of the community. And while traditional virtues may vary from the austerity of Spartan society to the openness of modern America, their intent is to create cohesiveness within the society or institution.

In *Laws*, considered Plato's most political writing, he tells the parable of the Athenian stranger with the stranger saying "let our race be something that is not lowly, then, if that is what you cherish, but worthy of a certain seriousness."[10] Many, however, using a Platonic metaphor, can only "stare realty in the face [and] the truth is too strong for most eyes."[11] A natural response to this has been expressed philosophically through the use of esotericism and ritual. Ritual, which is natural in form and content, is often highly elaborate and filled with symbolism and allegory. Ritual tends to be celebratory in nature and is experienced at various levels through different senses. It can be a therapeutic and cathartic tool but it can also be a formula that enables us to interpret our drives and motivations in term of brotherly love and affection as it inculcates in us respect for our traditions and beliefs. It is not necessarily to be understood, however, but rather to be felt and experienced. Ritual is a celebration of life and its experiences as well as of human striving and motivation. It may well be a higher route to the understanding of the human and the divine.

The esoteric tradition of Freemasonry is centered on the Temple of Solomon as described in I Kings and II Chronicles. The duty of the apprentice is to carry the stone hewn and finished by the fellow craft to the building site. The Temple reminds the initiate that he is to build a temple "within his heart" with the same degree of perfection as that given to the original Temple at Jerusalem. The Temple esoterically represents the center and the state of the universe. It was built on a high place, a mountain, a traditional center for worship as well as the earthly home of the Deity. The building was raised on a mountain so as to be both spiritual and temporal. The universal temple alluded to in Masonic degrees represents esoterically, then, not only the physical structure but also that of man as well as a mystical temple to be constructed through moral labor within the individual heart. Its construction (or continued reconstruction) must be the work of men who use the "living stones" of their conscience to realize God's power and unity.

In Freemasonry, notes William Burkle, there are a number of characteristics exhibited by its members: socialite, historian, ritualists, symbolists, and charitable. Esoteric Freemasonry is not for all members, any more than is any other single function of the Craft. This does not mean that it is any more or less important than any other path, but rather that it a discipline to which few are truly inclined. Esoteric Freemasons tend to converse with like-minded Brothers in limited numbers, but this is not to suggest that a thorough understanding of esotericism's contributions to the Craft are to be explored only by an elite few. It behooves all Brothers who truly seek "Light" through Freemasonry to study not only our traditions, principles, ritual, allegories, and ethics, but also to consider well the method by which they are transmitted—esotericism.

NOTES

1. Beata Megyesi, "Copiale cipher. Translation from German (August 2011), p. 69, located at https://stp.lingfil.uu.se/~bea/copiale/copiale-translation.pdf.

2. Francis Bacon, The *Advancement of Learning,* edited by G.W Kitchin (Philadelphia, Paul Dry Books, 2001), 132-133.

3. Arthur Melzer, *Philosophy between the Lines: The Lost History of Exoteric Writing,* (Chicago: The University of Chicago Press, 2014), 16.

4. Melzer, *Philosophy between the Lines.* 16.

5. Melzer, *Philosophy between the Lines,* 17.

6. Reinhart Kosselleck, *Critique and Crisis: Enlightenment and the Pathogenesis of Modern Society* (Oxford, UK: Berg, 1988), 62.

7. Isadore Twersky (ed.), *Miishnab Torah, Bkk. 1,* in *A Maimonides Reader* (New York: Behrman House, 1972), 47.

8. Melzer, *Philosophy Between the Lines,* 167.

9. R.W. Dyson (ed.), *Augustine: The City of God against the Pagans.* (Cambridge UK: Cambridge University Press, 1998), 960.

10. Plato, *The Laws of Plato,* Thomas Pangle (trans.). (Chicago: The University of Chicago Press, 1980), 194.

11. Melzer, *Philosophy Between the Lines,* 190.

Chapter Seven

Ritual Interpreted

All meanings depend on the key of interpretation.
—George Eliot

Figure 7.1.   Masonic ritual 4.

An excellent way to begin interpreting Masonic ritual is to examine the specific *Bible* passages recited during the circumambulation in each degree. In the Entered Apprentice Degree Psalm 133 is used to demonstrate unity. The Fellow Craft Degree utilizes Amos 7 to show that God has measured His people as He does all people and found them warped thus worthy of correction or plumbing. And in the Master Mason Degree, Ecclesiastes or The Preacher, the kindly cynic, provides those willing to listen a description of the passage from youth to age in what is generally accepted to be one of the most moving passages in literature and is often compared to the best of Marcus Aurelius' *Meditations* and Pascal's *Thoughts*.

Psalm 133 begins with a declaration of the usefulness of unity informing us that it is better to function together than with divisiveness. In the ancient Hebrew *gam shenayim* implies the goodness of those who are of the same belief system to be united for a sacred purpose. And that this unity is best accomplished within a sacred space or "same place." This passage was part of the initiation of the Knights Templar and is quoted by St. Augustine as Divine authority for monastic life. The passage further admonishes us that we are brethren not only through nature and "blood," but also through our common social and personal interactions. The mutual love described is that referred to in the New Testament as *agape* described most eloquently and emotionally in I Corinthians 13.

The entire passage demonstrates that we cannot say too much about the necessity of persuading people to live together in peace and harmony and suggests that those who abide by this admonition will receive God's blessing and approval. "How good" states the passage, how proper it is to promote happiness by the diffusion of good influences through the broad spectrum of brotherhood. How pleasant and filled with delight is the mind so engaged. And though the brethren will separate and go into their homes—to their scattered habitations—it is always most pleasant to see them assembled in harmony and unity. This unity, implies the passage, will have an important influence upon the world resulting in a reduction of strife and contention.

The "precious ointment" suggests not only consecration, but also an infusion of knowledge through that act to the lowest members of the society. Brotherly love, we are then told, does not diffuse its blessing unless it descends to all assembled. The implication of the passage is that if we love one another in unity and fellowship, immortality will follow. The cost of the ointment was not small, it being composed of some of the most precious spices: myrrh, cinnamon, calamus, cassia and olive oil. Yet as is the dew, it is freely given and descends from the highest mountain to the lowest valley. The brotherly love demonstrated through the unity described in the passage is rare and is not the kind of affection that comes and goes. It represents a perfect union. We are brothers together not because of some genetic bond, but rather by a combination of commonwealth and an attachment to the same ancient Fraternity.

In the Second Degree, Amos, the shepherd-prophet of righteousness, preaches "harsh words in a smooth season."[1] He points out to Israel their failings in social dealings and their shallow piety. The man from Tekoa articulates his encounters with the Deity—*YHWH*—and his successful intervention on behalf of Israel. Amos presents a conservative interpretation by condemning ritual as a futile exercise unless it is accompanied by ethical dealings among men. The book itself is considered a religious text of the highest order in which the audience participates in the cosmic drama directly and indirectly. Some scholars speculate that much of the book was intended to be a form of congregational reading or hymn with the leader asking the questions and the people answering in unison. It is also worthy of note that in Amos 5:8 reference is made to "the seven stars" or the Pleiades which are part of Masonic symbolism and often represented on tracing boards, floor cloths, and other Masonic iconography.

Amos utilizes what is best described as the subterfuge of entrapment and is compared to II Samuel 12 where David is given a case to judge in which he pronounces a death sentence for the theft of sheep only to be rebuked by the prophet Nathan who reveals the subterfuge and declares David equally guilty for the death of Uriah and adultery with Bathsheba. The rhetorical trap is set in the first two chapters and, though subtle, is directed at the audience or reader. Amos declares that he will intervene on Israel's behalf which is, itself, a trap since he has now eliminated the possibility of reconciliation with *YHWH*. The trap is then revealed and the lion's roar, which is a metaphor for divine speech, turns into prophecy. The trap has forced the audience to judge their relationship with the Deity and sets the stage for chapters seven, eight, and nine.

Chapters seven through nine may be considered as relatively independent from the remainder of the book. The emphasis is now on Amos and his interaction with *YHWH*. They are recounted in the first person with some of the verses, specifically Amos 7: 10-17, being a possible later addition. The visions of Amos recounted in Chapter 7 are virtually identical beginning with the words "Thus the lord *YHWH* showed me." For Freemasons, the critical verses are those describing the third vision which begins with "Behold, my Lord was standing on a wall of *anak* [possibly tin or lead] and in his hand [was] *anak* [tin?]." The passage describes how the sanctuaries will be destroyed yet foreshadows the reconciliation between *YHWH* and Israel.

This passage employs some of the most intricate and esoteric word-play in the Old Testament. What was *anak?* The word is used nowhere else in *The Bible* and has been interpreted to mean "tin," "lead", and, most commonly, "plumb" referring to the lead weight on a plumb-line. There are multiple layers of symbolism inherent in the word and its use in these verses. Tin and lead are both soft, malleable metals virtually useless unless alloyed with other metals such as copper to create bronze. In Amos, the meaning of the word appears to shift with context. Defined as "tin" it is a metaphor for the suffering to be inflicted on Israel and yet *YHWH* appears to set Amos (also represented as tin) among the people to "set them straight." There is also a suggestion that "tin" is incapable of standing alone and requires intervention or mixing with something stronger—possibly the Deity. The word *anak* displays a rich interplay within the language in which the repetition of a word can result in its transformation. Its use is reminiscent of the multi-layered symbolism prevalent in Freemasonry.

The circumambulation of the Third or Master Mason Degree utilizes Ecclesiastes 12 to demonstrate the fate of all mankind. The book of Ecclesiastes is often treated as either a depressing litany of the futilities of life, or as a simplistic series of homilies, warning people to avoid things in life that might seem good because they are really bad ("vain"). The great, triumphant, enlightening truth of Ecclesiastes is treated, all too often, as only a slim ray of hope. Ecclesiastes is, however, the only book of pure philosophy in *The Bible*. It's the only one needed, because it considers, however briefly, the entire human condition, and provides the answer to human existence, thus rendering further speculations somewhat unnecessary.

Ecclesiastes 12:1-14
"Remember now thy Creator in the days of thy youth, while the evil days come not, nor the years draw nigh, when thou shalt say, I have no pleasure in them;
While the sun, or the light, or the moon, or the stars, be not darkened, nor the clouds return after the rain:
In the day when the keepers of the house shall tremble, and the strong men shall bow themselves, and the grinders cease because they are few, and those that look out of the windows be darkened,
And the doors shall be shut in the streets, when the sound of the grinding is low,
and he shall rise up at the voice of the bird, and all the daughters of music shall be brought low;
Also when they shall be afraid of that which is high, and fears shall be in the way,
and the almond tree shall flourish, and the grasshopper shall be a burden, and desire shall fail:
Because man goes to his long home, and the mourners go about the streets:
Or ever the silver cord is loosed, or the golden bowl be broken, or the pitcher be broken at the fountain, or the wheel broken at the cistern,
Then shall the dust return to the earth as it was:
and the spirit shall return unto God who gave it."[2]

In this last chapter of Ecclesiastes, the argument is made that our dependence upon God and our seeking of significance in Him rather than in that which is "under the sun" is a very personal quest. The author's words are intended to head off the mid-life crisis men face as they begin to recognize their limitations and inabilities. The text describes growing older as a natural process during which limitations and inabilities will creep into our lives emphasizing that this is normal. It is the course and the cost of life. To fight it is to be distracted by it. We must take what God gives us today, appreciate it, and enjoy it.

The Preacher is desperately searching for significance as he grows older and has exhausted all the means by which man can find significance under the sun--including wisdom. He becomes wiser only by acknowledging *the whole duty of man is to "Fear God, and keep his commandments."* There is no wisdom under the sun that can allow man to *understand* God, yet, in Chapter 11 the Preacher informs us that the man who lives peaceably and in harmony with others, *even the unbeliever*, will enjoy much in life. But even the unbeliever is admonished to remember that life is short and that the Lord provides an eternal solution given through the Preacher in Chapter 12.

SYMBOLISM IN CHAPTER 12

Keepers of the house: hands
The strong men: legs
The grinders: teeth
Those who look out the windows: eyes
The doors: ears
Sound of grinding low: a person gets older he works less and misses the pleasures of that work
Rise up at the voice of birds: rising up early as do the elderly, not able to sleep late
Daughters of music brought low: hard of hearing
Afraid of that which is high: fear of falling
Almond tree: white blossoms, the white hair
Grasshopper a burden: too weak to carry a burden
Desire shall fail: sex drive wanes
Long home: eternity

Thus in Ecclesiastes 12 we see two pictures of death. The first is a silver cord holding a golden bowl in which a flame (light) burns which represents a lamp in the Ancient world. The cord breaks, the bowl is shattered, the light goes out. Death has occurred. The second image is of water, symbolic of life, becoming unavailable or drained away. The pitcher which holds the water is shattered, a physical parallel of death. Then the wheel by which water is drawn is broken which is interpreted to refer to the heart pumping the blood through the body. It no longer works, it is broken, death is the result. These stark images are drawn to motivate us to realize that we might spend our lives trying to find something that will never be found and in doing so come to death's door realizing we could have had so much more if we had only depended upon Divine inspiration and guidance.

In the final picture, death returns us to creation. "Then shall the dust [body] return to the earth as it was: and the spirit [he life of man] shall return unto God who gave it."[3] is a direct parallel to the creation of man account found in Genesis 2:7. Prior to giving his final verdict on the matter of significance in life, the Preacher establishes how he came to this conclusion. Experience is not the best teacher, he tells us. Personal experience of failure can show us what is wrong but is cannot show us what is right. Experience is limited to that which is under the sun, to that which is earth bound. Experience can show us things as being better but it cannot show us absolute best. It is similar to natural revelation in that it shows us our inability, our weakness, our smallness, but not always our greatness. Experience can show us that there is a God who is far beyond man, but experience alone cannot lead us to God's love and God's wisdom.

Knowledge in Hebrew is the word *DAR-ATH* and includes perception, skill, and wisdom. Ecclesiastes teaches us how to apply these principles of knowledge to daily life in which truth is to be pondered, searched out, and properly arranged. The passage further teaches us to weigh ourselves on a scale to find the best truth. The Preacher searched outside of himself to reach his conclusion: "For God shall bring every work into judgment, with every secret thing, whether it be good, or whether it be evil."[4]

The Second or Fellow Craft degree includes, in addition to the reading from Amos, the story of Jephthah as recounted in The Book of Judges Chapter 11. The story, which is included in the Winding Stairs' Lecture, is there, most probably, because it is the only biblical account of the use of a password, but it possesses for Freemasons a deeper, more personal meaning. The story is in the form of a personal history and a vow made by that person to the Deity. A vow is an oath, with the Deity being both the witness and recipient of the promise. A religious vow indicates that the petitioner's piety and spiritual attitude outweigh all other considerations.

Jephthah, a "mighty warrior" of the Tribe of Gilead, is described as "the son of a harlot." He is driven out of the tribe by his half-brothers and goes to the land of Tod in the region of Ammon (as in Ammonites) where he associates with "worthless [also translated as 'empty'] fellows." When the Ammonites make war on Israel, Jephthah is called home to be their leader. He is promised that when he defeats the Ammonites, his position will become permanent. To achieve victory and to seal his place as "Judge over Israel, he vows that "If thou shalt without fail deliver the children of Ammon into mine hands, then it shall be, that whatsoever cometh forth of the doors of my house to meet me, when I return in peace from the children of Ammon, shall surely be the Lords, and I will offer it up for a burnt sacrifice."[5] The Ammonites are defeated and upon his return, Jephthah is met first by his daughter, his only child, but he is bound by his vow to God: "For I have opened my mouth unto the Lord, and I cannot go back."[6] The vow is then fulfilled.

As with the recitation of Psalm 133, Amos 7, and Ecclesiastes 12, an understanding of the deeper, symbolic, esoteric meaning is essential to a full understanding of Masonic ritual. It is easy to lose the lessons offered in the horror of human sacrifice, but the story speaks to us of equality; the importance of carefully considering oaths (words); the implication of keeping one's word; and the necessity of being ever watchful and thoughtful about what we say, think, and do as well as how we treat others based on preconceived notions. Jephthah was "thrust out," and, though surrounded by "worthless fellows," he creates a personal reputation such that when threatened by the Ammonites, the elders of Israel bring him back to be their leader. This teaches us that we are not bound by birth, but that we have within us the God-given ability to overcome even the most appalling circumstances and achieve by our own merits.

The story of Jephthah goes further, though, and teaches us that by overcoming and forsaking poor associations and replacing them with better companions, we demonstrate our reevaluation of our life's purpose and our place in society. The story further reminds us of the power of an oath or vow, especially when made to the Deity. We can easily break a vow or oath if we assume it has no meaning. Jephthah, though, reflects upon the meaning of the oath and to whom given, and his spirituality outweighs all other concerns as it should with Masons. We, and he, are admonished to consider our tendency to speak before well considering our words; to think in narrow ways; or to act in a manner that is not pleasing to God or man.

Freemasonry teaches us overtly to subdue our passions, to reflect upon our thoughts and words, and to take action only after careful consideration. It also teaches us that an oath once taken is for an indefinite period and covers all situations. Had Jephthah more wisely considered his words, he may not have been forced to exclaim: "Alas, my daughter! Thou hast brought me very low, and thou art one of them that trouble me: for I have opened my mouth unto the Lord, and I cannot go back."[7]

TO MAKE A MASON

The ritual used to "make a Mason" has evolved significantly since the beginnings of Accepted Freemasonry at the end of the sixteenth century. The earliest record of the initiation of a non-operative Mason, as noted previously, is found in the minutes of the Lodge of Edinburgh at St. Mary's Chapel dated July 1634 but no details are given and before the second decade of the eighteenth century, no reference is to be found to three separate degrees. "Making a Brother" or "Making a Free Mason" are the only words used. The process, based upon existing records, drawings, and diaries, was simple. A description of the process may be found in Chapter I.

To summarize, however, when the candidate was received into the Lodge, he took an obligation on the Volume of Sacred Law to preserve the *MYS-TERIES* not the secrets of the Craft. The various recognition words and signs were communicated to him, usually by his sponsor who also served as his instructor and mentor. A charge was given informing the new Mason of his duty to God, his master, his Brothers, and his fellow men. A history of the Craft was generally read. It should be noted that in none of these manuscripts is there a reference to the Hiramic Legend. In its place was heard the Legend of Noah as used by Antediluvium or Noachida Masons with the most complete versions of the Noah story found in the Cooke Manuscript of 1410 and the Graham manuscript of the early 1700s.

The dark anteroom noted in Chapter I became The Chamber of Reflection which had a close parallel in the bed chamber occupied by those about to be crowned King of England beginning in the late 1270s. When Henry III renovated the Palace at Westminster he directed his royal painters to create a coronation scene on the wall directly behind the bed which depicted Edward the Confessor being crowned by a bevy of Bishops. On either side of the great bed were depicted Solomon's guard standing watch. These murals were intended to cause Henry's son, Edward I, as well as future kings, to reflect upon the Confessor's example as a wise, just, and devoted ruler, as well as upon the wisdom displayed by Solomon. The depiction of virtues conquering vices gave visual instructions on the proper way to live. In 1292 Edward I added to these wall-paintings new murals which depicted scenes from *The Bible*, mostly taken from the Book of Maccabees, alluding to the fate of the Christian communities in the Holy Land. All of these paintings were intended to begin the thinking process necessary for all future rulers of England as well as on the ways of war and peace and on the demands of kinghood.

The Chamber of Reflection is not used in all Lodges, being most prevalent among Ancient Free and Accepted Masons in Mexico, Central and South America, Europe, and in some degrees in the Scottish, and York Rites. It is generally defined as "a small room adjoining the Lodge, in which, preparatory to initiation, the candidate is enclosed for the purpose of indulging in serious mediation which its somber appearance and the gloomy emblems with which it is furnished are calculated to produce."[8] The furnishing generally include a skull, bread and water, an hourglass, and various saying. The candidate is given paper and pen and asked to write a philosophical statement that includes his moral philosophy and an elaboration on his reasons for becoming a Freemason. He may even be asked specific questions to which there are no right or wrong answers, but are to be answered based on his personal and personal experiences. At some point later, his essay may be given back to him and he may be asked to comment on his answers. A candle and mirror are also prominent accoutrements to the room. The lessons taught there are that initiation is an individual internal process. No external source can transform a man; he can only do it for himself.

As previously discussed, Lodges at this time did not have permanent homes and typically utilized an upper room at a local tavern or public place for their meetings. Some Lodges met in private homes or, even, academic buildings. Church buildings were not typically used by Lodges. This lack of a permanent home required that all accoutrements of the Fraternity be portable.

The candidate's circumambulation about the Lodge room symbolically represented, and still does, his journey from darkness to light. He was led to the altar, given the obligation, kissed the Volume of Sacred Law and said "*fune merum genio*" which is Latin for "pour out the good wine for our pleasure." Since the trestle board or feasting board is already in place, the brothers drank a toast given by the Master to the "heart that conceals and to the tongue that never reveals." After which everyone drew their glasses, now empty, across their throats. Instruction began with an explanation of the floor pattern and the emblems on the tracing board were expounded upon much as they are in modern lectures. At this point, the new Brother assumed his position at the end of the line and, bucket and pail in hand, was instructed to "wash away" the figures on the floor, retire to the preparation room, recover his valuables, and return to the lodge. An etching by William Hogarth, though intended to spoof the Gormogons, depicts the apprentice, bucket and pail in hand.

At the conclusion of the gathering, the Craft assembled in a circle, hands joined crossways to form a chain, right over left, and ended the ceremony. Feasting and toasting followed accompanied reciting information for the Apprentice in the form of a catechism with the Master asking the questions. Each brother could propose a toast as he desired upon answering a question. If a brother did not know the answer to the Master's question, he would stand, clap his hands, place his right hand on his left breast, give a very low bow, usually take a drink, and pass the question to the next brother in line. The lodge was closed by the Senior Warden.

A Lodge of Freemasons is open only after being properly tyled with each officer reciting his place in the room as well as his duties. An open Lodge signifies that the Mysteries (esoteric ritual and philosophy) and Secrets (mainly recognition signs) of Freemasonry may now be freely and openly revealed and discussed. In degree work, the Lodge is opened "in due form" and the Master instructs that the candidate be properly prepared and, possibly, left for reflection, a time-honored tradition. To gain entrance the candidate or his proposer makes a symbolic set of knocks at the door similar to the knocks delivered at the cathedral door upon the initiation of a novice or the ordination of a priest. The candidate, note Duncan and Webb as well as modern Masonic monitors, is asked a series of questions before and after he is granted admission into the Lodge. And, as already noted, an obligation not an oath is taken. Each degree follows basically the same format with lectures varying significantly until the allegory is completed. Early Masons often engaged in songs during the degrees and some ancient monitors include those for the Fellow Craft and Master Mason Degree. Non-degree work is markedly similar with virtually identical opening and closing rituals as well as a display of the signs, but without the recitation of the complete obligation and the explanations given in the lectures.

The Master Mason Degree within the symbolic lodges appears to have been a development within the Grand Lodge of England at some point after 1725. Most Freemasons remained Fellow Crafts all of their days and it is not until 1777 that the first and second degrees are noted as having been given on different evenings. It is possible that a separate third or Master Mason degree was worked in some Lodge by invitation only, but Bro. George Bell, for example, was a Fellow Craft when he served as Deputy Grand Master in 1751.

The core allegory of Freemasonry is the Building of King Solomon's Temple at Jerusalem, but the Hiramic Legend is not history, rather it is a ritualistic expression of the type of conflict the human soul experiences while "traveling though this vail of tears." Hiram's labor was that of organization and direction just as modern Freemasons labor to supervise, organize, and direct our lives and actions. The story of Hiram is not an artificial misfortune; it is not about savagery or "boys will be boys." Its concerns are human dignity and integrity, major components of the human soul. It is an allegory, a symbol, of what happens in every man's life and demonstrates that defeat can lead to elevation and mastery. The legend is not generally explained nor propounded upon in depth and therefore seldom discussed in open Lodge. The reason for this is simple: it is something each person must learn for himself. This is not to imply, however, that the allegory is not worthy of in-depth exploration, contemplation, and discussion. It is a sublime tragedy, a "mystery" of Freemasonry that requires the ritualists, the candidate, and the brethren to commit themselves heart, soul, and mind to its reenactment. It promulgates to all involved the nature of the eternal quest found in all great mysteries. And though the "word" remains elusive, it is the search or the quest that is paramount.

All modern Freemasons are fully knowledgeable about the Legend of Hiram, at least at a superficial level, and its place as the dominant allegory of the Craft. Few, however, are familiar with its predecessor, the Legend of Noah, therefore it is included in its entirety below for comparison, contrast, and edification.

THE LEGEND OF NOAH ACCORDING TO GRAHAM 1725 [9]

Shem ham and jepheth ffor to go their father
noahs grave for to try if they could find anything about him ffor to lead them
to the valuable secret which this famieous preacher had for I hop all will
allow that all things needful for the new world was in the ark with noah
Now these 3 men had already agreed that if they did not find the very thing
If self that the first thing what they found was to be to them as a secret they not
doubting but did most ffirmly believe than God was able and would also prove
willing through their faith prayer and obedience for to cause what they did
find for to prove as vertuable to them as if they had received the secret at
ffirst from God himself at its head spring so came to the Grave finding
nothing save the dead body all most consumed away takeing a
greip at a ffinger
it came away so from Joynt to Joynt so to the wrest so to the Elbow so they
Reared up the dead body and supported it setting ffoot to ffoot knee to knee
Breast to breast Cheeck to cheeck and hand to back and cryed out
help o ffather as if they had said o ffathter of heaven helpo us no Earthly
ffather
cannot so Laid down the dead body again and now knowing what
to do – so one said is et marrow in this bone and the second said but a
dry bone and the third said it stinketh so they agreed for to give it a name
as is known to free masonry to this day so went to their undertakings
and afterwards works stood: et it is to believen and allso understood that
the virtue did not proceed from what they ffound or how it was called but
ffrom ffaith and prayer o thu it continued the will pass for the deed.

The Legend of Noah involves the same quest for something that was lost as well as the raising up of a body and the implication for all humanity of the necessity of passing to future generations the wisdom of the past. A careful reading of this Legend and its comparison to that of Hiram is worthy of any dedicated Freemason.

SYMBOLISM IN MASONIC ARCHITECTURE AND FURNISHING

The form of a Lodge is a parallelopipedon (a prism whose bases are parallelograms) with its symbolic length extending indefinitely from east to west; its breadth from north to south; and its depths from the surface of earth to its core and, as demonstrated in Jacob's Ladder, as high as the heavens which form its starry covering. A Lodge is supported by three great pillars situated east, west, and south which metaphorically demonstrate the three principles of wisdom, strength and beauty (Greek designations for Ionic, Doric and Corinthian). These pillars are located at the stations of the principle officers with wisdom in the east, strength in the west, and beauty in the south.

A Lodge is covered only by heaven or a "clouded canopy" which extends from horizon to horizon and beyond thus covering all mankind. This heaven usually includes stars, the Deity's magnificent representations in the night sky, and is often colored blue emblematical of trust, loyalty, wisdom, confidence, intelligence, faith, truth, and heaven. Blue is also considered beneficial to mind and body because it slows human metabolism and produces a calming effect thus resulting in harmony and unity among the Brethren. Immediately under the physical covering of the lodge is a beautiful variegated and checkered flooring which points out the diversity of objects which decorate and adorn creation, the animate as well as the inanimate, and symbolizes, as well, human life, checkered with good and evil.

Above the floor and central to the heavens, is located the sun or blazing star--the center, which lights and enlightens the earth and by its often benign influence bestows its blessing on mankind in general. The blazing star at center also alludes to the Almighty, overshadowing us with his Divine love as he distributes His blessing to all who receive His light.

The border which surrounds the checkered pavement is symbolical of the relationship of man to the Deity and to each other, thus emphasizing the unity of the whole—the Divine world and the terrestrial world. Resting solidly on the pavement is the altar which holds the Great Lights, The Volume of Sacred Law which rules and governs our faith and practice, and on which all are obligated. The square and compasses rest on the Sacred Law and, when thus united, teach us to regulate our live and actions; to act upon the square; to circumscribe our desires; and to control our passions. The square and compasses may be mechanical tools used in everyday labor, but they symbolize our moral duty. They work in the real and spiritual world to bring rude matter—human beings--into due, true, and perfect form.

Surrounding the altar in some manner (based on jurisdiction and tradition) are the three lesser lights. Traditionally they were burning tapers placed there to represent the sun, moon, and Worshipful Master with the taper symbolizing the Sun in the south, the moon in the west, and the Worshipful Master in the east. Modern fire and insurance regulations have replace burning tapers with some form of electronic illumination, but the symbolism remains. There are twelve different patterns in use in the United States with some jurisdictions placing the lights immediately in front or of at the stations of the Worshipful Master, the Senior Warden, and the Junior Warden. In ancient lodges they were the only candles in the Lodge thus the only light. The absence of a light in the north is symbolic of King Solomon's Temple relationship to the ecliptic and thus Masonically deemed a place of darkness.

Every Lodge labors under a charter or warrant issued upon application to the Grand Lodge of that Jurisdiction. The charter symbolizes a regularly constituted Lodge of Freemasons. In many older Lodges, the Charter hanging on the wall is a duplicate issued by the Grand Lodge of that Jurisdiction with the original being deposited in that Grand Lodge's archives. The Charter or its duplicate must always be on display in the East. Most Lodges also display within the Lodge room photographs of past Masters as well as the current Master and, in some cases, the Wardens. Other pictures or paintings are often of George Washington or other Masonic notables.

Situated also in the East, West, and South are three pedestals which represent the three great columns and are utilized by the principle officers as podiums. These columns are traditionally carved in the Ionic, Doric, and Corinthian style with that at the Master's station being Ionic, the Senior Warden's being Doric, and the Junior Warden's being Corinthian. The Ionic symbolizes wisdom and is traditionally said to have been formed after the model of an agreeable young woman thus representing temperance and stability—traits all Worshipful Masters should possess. The Doric column, which is plain and natural, sits in the West and represents strength inherent in its simplicity. It is also the foundation for the other orders and symbolically is intended to support with strength the wisdom inherent in the Ionic. The Corinthian is the richest of the five orders. It is stately and superb in design and construction. It sits in the South and denotes the beauty of the day as well as the passage of time.

In front of the Worshipful Master in the East sit the Rough Ashlar and the Perfect Ashlar. The Rough Ashlar is an unfinished, rude, imperfect stone which alludes to our basic nature which, without hewing and virtuous education, is incapable of performing its assigned task. The Perfect Ashlar, symbolizes the results of the work of both operative and speculative Masons. It has now achieved a state of perfection which enables it to fit exactly within the structure thus performing a unity of purpose. When coupled with its lifting tool, the Lewis (seldom represented in Lodges in the United States), it denotes strength through perfection. It bears the burden; it meets the need; it also denotes the privilege of serving our fellow man.

Each officer in the Lodge wears a jewel which is assigned to his station. The Square, which symbolizes morality, is around the neck of the Worshipful Master. It is presented to the Entered Apprentice as one of the Three Great Lights and as the official emblem of the Worshipful Master; to the Fellow Craft as one of his working tools; and to the Master Mason as emblematical of how all Masons should part—upon the square. It is also to be found engraved on the Master's pedestal and often on the east side of the Altar. The Level, which is similar to the plumb but used to mark horizontal surfaces rather than perpendiculars is assigned to the Senior Warden. It symbolizes "the level" and admonishes us that regardless of our social or economic status, we are all "traveling on the level of time toward that undiscovered country." It is also engraved on the Senior Warden's pedestal; and adorns the west side of the Altar. All Masons should meet upon the level. The Plumb determines if the wall is vertical and reminds us of upright conduct— "walking uprightly before God and man." It is the jewel of the Junior Warden; is engraved on his pedestal; and is on the south side of the Altar. Masons should act by the plumb.

In all regular Lodges is represented a point within a circle located between two perpendicular parallel lines and at the vertex of the circle is found the Volume of Sacred Law. The point in the middle of the circle is an ancient astrological sign that represents the Earth as the center of the universe. It now represents the individual Brother—the center of the Lodge. The parallel lines originally represented the summer and winter solstices so important to agricultural societies and denoted the times for planting and harvesting. In about 300 A.D., the Christian Church made June 24 and December 27 feast days for St. John the Baptist and St. John the Evangelist, referred to in Masonic ritual as early patron saints of Freemasonry. The lines are now said to represent the attributes of those Saints. And the Volume of Sacred Law teaches us the proper balance between our desires and knowledge through virtuous education.

Other symbols found in the Lodge are the twenty-four-inch gauge which teaches us to measure work, family, refreshment, and service to God and man in appropriate proportions. The setting maul or common gavel symbolizes the divestment of our "hearts and consciences of the vices and superfluities" of daily life thus enabling us to focus on the Deity's plan for mankind and our place in it. Jacob's Ladder, taken from Genesis 28, teaches us to have "faith in God, hope in immortality and charity toward all mankind, but the greatest is charity." The other rungs of the ladder symbolize fortitude, prudence, temperance and justice, the four cardinal virtues. The key, usually suspended below the ladder by the thread of life symbolizes the passage of words between the guttural and pectoral and their connection with the heart. It is the key to the index of the mind intended to prevent us from uttering anything but what the heart and mind truly dictate. It is not made of metal, though, it is "the tongue of good report."

The Worshipful Master's station is elevated three steps above the lodge room floor; the Senior Warden's two steps; and the Junior Warden's one step. These symbolize the three principles stages of human life—youth, manhood, and age, and also demonstrate the Riddle of the Sphinx which relates to the same three phases. The two great pillars labeled Boaz and Jachin (See I Kings 6 – 7; II Chronicles 2 – 4) may be found framing the door from the preparation room or the Senior Warden's station. They are also represented by columns sitting on the pedestals at the stations of the Senior and Junior Wardens with Boaz in the West and Jachin in the South. Tradition dictates that while the Lodge is at Labor, Boaz is standing erect and Jachin at ease, with the reverse being true when the Lodge is closed.

Each Masonic Degree has a dedicated biblical passage: Psalm 133 for the Entered Apprentice Degree; Amos Chapter Seven for the Fellow Craft Degree; and Ecclesiastes Chapter Twelve for the Master Mason Degree(see explanations above). Each degree candidate is properly clothed to include a Cable Tow which anciently represented the distance a person could walk in three hours or his obligation to his fellow man. It is now purely symbolic. The actual length of a cable tow in England is about 800 feet and references the cable used to pull barges in inland canals. This is not to be confused with the Cable Length which is three-hundred and thirty feet in Spanish measure and six-hundred and sixty feet in English measure representing the length of rope or chain connected to an anchor.

Candidates are traditionally presented into the Lodge barefoot as referenced in the Book of Ruth: "a man plucked off his shoe." This custom does not refer to the law about refusing to marry a brother's widow, but was usual in the transfer of inheritances: for in Ruth the relative was not a brother, but simply a kinsman; and the shoe was not pulled off by Ruth, but by the kinsman himself. In other traditions it is the right glove that is exchanged this confirming the custom that when we purchase anything new, it is customary to give something in exchange. As noted in Chapter IV, candidates for reception into various holy orders are also barefoot.

These symbols were and are found in regular Masonic Lodges and often displayed on Tracing Boards for the purpose of instruction. The process of making a mason or the ritual was simple, at first, and became more involved, expanding to Three Symbolic Lodge Degrees and numerous appendant degrees over time. The Lodge moved from a transient nature to having a permanent home and with that the symbols and patterns were no longer, of necessity, transportable. And detailed lectures and illustrations in books replaced Tracing Boards which had become extremely elaborate over time and have now assumed a status as pieces of art as have many Masonic Temples which have been awarded the status of architectural masterpieces worthy of preservation and, even, designation as national treasures.

NOTES

1. "The Book of Amos." *The Oxford Annotated Bible*.(New York: Oxford University Press, 1962), 1107.
2. Authorized or King James Version, *Holy Bible.*
3. Ecclesiastes, 12:7.
4. Ecclesiastes, 12:14.
5. Judges, 11:30-31.
6. Judges, 11:35.
7. Judges, 11:35.
8. Helio L. Da Costa Jr. "The Chamber of Reflection." Located at http://freemasonry.bcy.ca/texts/ Gmd1999/pondering.html. Retrieved, October 10, 2015.
9. *The Graham Manuscript*. Located at http://www.themasonictrowel.com/ebooks/freemasonry/eb0112.pdf. Retrieved, July 7, 2015.

Chapter Eight

What the Present and the Future May Hold

You are hereby summoned to attend the duties of your Lodge
at Masonic Hall, Halesowen, on Friday, the 5th day of December, 1958,
at 5.30 o'clock p.m.
The Officers of the Lodge are requested to be punctual in their attendance.
Dress: Dark Suit, Black Tie, White Gloves.
—Lapal Lodge No. 6031, 1958

Figure 8.1.   Stonemason's Yard by Canaletto, abt. 1725.

Just because we live in the twenty-first century, some three hundred years after the formal founding of speculative Freemasonry, it does not follow that Freemasonry must considerably change itself or adapt its fundamental practices or principles in order to "come into the modern age." Freemasonry has a significant place in the modern world by providing a place for philosophical and ethical exploration by "young" men, many in their early 60s who, now retired, have sufficient time to devote to the Craft. Of equal, and possibly greater importance, is the need to develop future generations of Freemasons and ensure the survival of the Fraternity by coming to a common understanding that the future rests with the young both in head and body, and that these "young" men must be encouraged to participate to the fullest extent possible in the institution.

Age with all of its experience is important, but it must not be allowed to exclude or deter chronologically and psychologically young men from being made Masons or from participating fully in the governance of their Lodges and Grand Lodges. We need to recognize that our organization has a purpose in the community and in larger society which is greater than the internal operations of a Lodge. If Freemasonry in 2066 is to flourish, it must act now to address the needs and yearnings of today's youth. It must invest in human potential and again recognize that our great allegory is that of a pilgrim's journey to enlightenment and fulfillment. What is essential to survival and growth is that the Fraternity practice externally what it proclaims internally. It is even more critical that its members demonstrate in their daily lives the values Freemasonry espouses and that the Fraternity directly addresses the lack of knowledge, vision, dedication, and moral standards demanded in previous generations. Gotthold Lessing writing between 1778 and 1780 noted the following about Freemasonry; "Their true deeds are their secrets. . . the true deeds of the Freemasons are so great, and so far-reaching, that whole centuries elapse before they can say 'This was their doing. . . the true deeds of Freemasons are aimed at making all that are commonly described as good deeds for the most part superfluous."[1] It should be no different in the twenty-first century. Lessing goes on in the "Ernst und Falk" dialogues to state that Freemasons have made it "part of their business to reduce as far as possible the divisions which so much alienate people from one another;" and that they admit into the order "every worthy man of the right disposition, *irrespective of nationality, irrespective of religion, and irrespective of social class* [emphasis added by author]." Then he has Falk say "The secret of Freemasonry, as I've already told you, is something which the Freemason *cannot* put into words, even if it were possible for him to *want* to do so."[2] Truth, Lessing writes, as all Freemasons know, is not about possession, it is about the quest, the earnest effort to obtain truth (light) is the true mark of a man and constitutes his legacy.

To reach fulfillment in the search for truth, Freemasons are required to turn outward as well as inward. It is easily argued that Freemasonry is more important today that it has been in its almost three hundred history notes Bondy Consulting in its report *The Future of Freemasonry* prepared for the United Grand Lodge of England. It provides, Bondy notes, a "unique combination of friendship, belonging, and structure"[3] which helps people live moral and ethical lives. There is little doubt, suggests Bondy, that there are too many myths, misperceptions, and downright falsehoods perpetuated through media which prevent young men from seeking membership. What is essential to survival, then, is that we, as Freemasons, do all we can to ensure that others have a fuller more complete understanding of the Craft and its purpose and that, as Lessing suggests, we "walk the walk and talk the talk" by allowing our true deeds to be our secrets. Thus the decision to seek membership will be based on knowledge founded in facts and positive perceptions not fantasy or media sensationalism.

Freemasonry, contradictory to myth, is a transparent organization. Our constitutions, bylaws, aims, and goals are published and available to all. For example, www.ugle.org.uk contains a wealth of information about the Fraternity as do all of the websites maintained by Grand Lodges in the United States as well as a large number of regular Masonic organizations such as the Masonic Society and others. In the Bondy study, published in 2012, it is noted that one in four young British men surveyed considered becoming a Freemason but demurred because they had reached the conclusion that "it's not for people like me." The same is probably true in the U.S. and elsewhere. Freemasonry traditionally is open to all men regardless of race, color, religion, political views, national origin, or social or economic standing. Freemasons truly "meet upon the level."

Many men, young and more mature, would probably seek membership if the Craft worked to encourage all Brothers to more fully express Masonic values within the community through their daily lives not just to dispel myths and misrepresentations perpetuated by media and other groups, but to demonstrate that Freemasons are true to their word and their principles. The year 2017 will be a mile-stone year for Speculative Freemasonry marking the 300th year of its formation in London. And while membership numbers are falling in some jurisdictions, they are remaining stable or are increasing in others. In the United Kingdom, Freemasonry is second only to the National Lottery in its support of charitable endeavors, and in the United States the Shrine Hospital System is among the best known and most respected medical facilities nationwide. But men do not become Freemasons just to be charitable, there are numerous over avenues for that endeavor. They become Freemasons for camaraderie, knowledge, ethical and moral instruction, and a desire to help themselves be better men. They enjoy being Freemasons and gain something from it, or they would not remain members for fifty or sixty years.

Freemasonry is wrongly considered and often persecuted as a "secret" organization rather than an affiliation with an altruistic, educational society. It provides a special bond for its members and life-long friendships are commonly forged between Brothers. At the heart of Freemasonry, though, is its ritual which provides structure, community, continuity, and familiarity as well as moral and spiritual guidance and useful knowledge. It is the ritual of Freemasonry that expresses itself as representative of daily life, and when the Fraternity loses its center—its ritual—it no longer reflects its cause for being.

During the nineteenth century and up to the early 1960s in the United States, the Masonic Lodge was the center of every town. It was a link to the past and the center of social, economic, educational, and cultural life. Lodges, which once served as a center for professionals to meet and exchange ideas, and where voice was commonly given to thoughts and ideas which encouraged intellectual development, lost their way at some point after 1960 and no longer reflected the desire of young men to advance themselves and their society.

The predicted demise of Freemasonry has not taken place, but there has been significant reduction in numbers and participation in the United States and other countries. The Masonic Service Association of North America reports that there were about 1.4 million Freemasons in the United States in 2009 and about 1.16 million in 2015—a seventeen percent decline over those years. The United Grand Lodge of England, according to Pantograph Printing & Stationers, had about 251,000 members in 2009 and by 2015 had declined to about 212,000 members—a little more than fifteen percent loss over the same period. The Grand Lodge of Florida (the author's jurisdiction) counted more than 80,000 members in 1980. In 2015 that number had dropped by half to about 40,000 with only about 39,000 paying dues; and for the period 2009-2015, The Grand Lodge of Florida experienced a loss of about eighteen percent—not significantly different from the U.S. or U.G.L.E. average. This marked reduction in membership may be attributed to several factors including a cultural change away from fraternal organizations and, as so many bemoan, a combination of lack of free time and "too many" other things to do. We suggest, however, that these are minor factors and that the more critical problems lie in the fact that our Lodges have lost their focus on ritualistic proficiency; have significantly reduced, if no eliminated, education and moral and spiritual instruction; have lost their sense of awe about our traditions and legacy; and have reached the perspective that Freemasonry may be an important part of our lives but of no more relevance than any other club.

Ritual has been since time immemorial at the center of Masonic practice. Through it we pass to future generations not only the history and wisdom of our Craft but we also provide moral instruction and sound ethical decision making guidance. We reestablish for our members the importance of ritual in daily life as a teaching and reflective tool. Each time ritual is trivialized or performed less than satisfactorily it "reflects discredit" upon those involved—both ritualists in doing no better and in spectators who accept such shoddy performance as the norm. To perform ritual as it should be done demands concentration, dedication, and an understanding of the message being transmitted. The man, young or more mature, who is unwilling to commit the time and effort to mastering even the most basic procedures of opening, closing, and degree work, not to speak of catechisms and lectures, has not demonstrated worthiness to be the Master of a Lodge and lead young Masons in "the paths of truth and justice." Men in the modern era dedicate themselves to their careers, to their families, to self-improvement, and to other aspects of their lives which they deem important. If Freemasonry is indeed important, it follows that it deserves the same dedication and commitment. Freemasonry, unlike virtually all other fraternal organizations, offers vast opportunities for personal growth, spiritual awareness, and moral development. For centuries it facilitated the making of productive, successful citizens because the membership viewed the Fraternity as being of "highest importance and profound significance" and demonstrated this in ritual proficiency.

Secondly, too many Lodges have lost their sense of spiritual and moral structure by neglecting sound Masonic education. Freemasonry is not and never has been a religion, but it does offer profound and significant depth to the meaning of life beyond the reality of surface appearance. For centuries it has based itself soundly in the most profound historical, philosophical, and cultural thinking of the era. Freemasons of past generations were encouraged to seek the significance of the Craft and to examine in great detail the meaning of its symbols, philosophy, history, ethics, and traditions. In modern Freemasonry this depth of philosophical and educational discussion and exploration has often been abandoned and even among Research Lodges, the focus is on antiquarianism not the richness of meaning inherent to the Fraternity.

Finally, the imagination and psychological imperative of Freemasonry has been lost to a wide-spread apathy among the membership. This apathy is marked most by a deep-seated refusal to change and a constant chorus of "that's not the way we did it in the past." Freemasonry made a significant difference in the founding of the United States and had marked influence on a variety of public activities because it offered sound moral guidance; led the way in the establishment of democratic government; and, more than any other organization, recognized the wisdom of *considering all men equal*. Too much of modern Freemasonry has seemingly turned away from these principles that made the Fraternity so great and have entered into a self-fulfilling thought pattern which can only lead to further decline.

This loss is directly reflected in a marked reduction in sincere, directed reflection upon the meaning of the Craft which has resulted in Freemasons losing respect for both our history and our legacy. They may wear the ring, even have a Masonic license plate on their car, and commonly call others 'Brother," but they no longer truly cherish their legacy because they do not understand it. They have not been given sound Masonic education in their Lodges nor have they been encouraged to engage in discussion with their Brothers about our legends, allegories, symbols, and philosophy. Education and reflection are among the most dynamic aspects of human life. All men strive to learn and gain new knowledge which, coupled with sharing the knowledge obtained, promotes a sense of loyalty and fraternity among all men.

Freemasonry is an existential philosophy in that it delves into the meaning of human existence. The modern world has given rise to significant doubt about the very nature of human activity including religion, politics, external authority, even the efficacy of morality. Prior assumptions are commonly challenged and conventions are being overthrown because of a lack of knowledge about past experiences and the reasons for tradition. Men of today do not just seek certificates for their wall; pins for their lapels; or a string of honorifics after their names. Instead they desire self-improvement, harmony, diversity, organization, conflict-resolution, moral guidance, and a path for self-improvement. They also seek a fraternal bond not commonly available in other organizations. Freemasonry fulfills the human impulse to "dwell in unity" and this is accomplished only when our ritual, our education, and our reflection lead others to find the reality that so many dedicated Masons in previous generations discovered when they were "made a Mason."

Freemasonry must not follow the way of the Odd Fellows and strip our Lodges of ritual, catechism, education, and, yes, memorization. Masonic education must again become the focus of Masonic activity. It is that which sets us apart from all the clubs, orders, and other societies. The way to enlightenment as well as to the revitalization of Freemasonry in the twenty-first century is through sound, dedicated, Masonically educated leadership which is devoted to the Craft and to keeping it important in our lives as well as the life of our community and nation. At the same time, Freemasonry should not become the only driving force in human life. It is essential to balance our lives and our commitment to the craft. Freemasonry is not just the way we conduct ourselves in our Lodges, it is much more critically how we conduct ourselves at home, in our careers, and in our communities. This is what marks us as "full-time" Masons who "walk the walk" not just "talk the talk." Our deeds are our true secrets.

So whence does Freemasonry proceed? A review of the Pew Research Center analysis of the millennial generation (those born between 1981 and 1996 and thus prime candidates for membership in Masonic Lodges) provides insight that can guide Masonic revitalization. The report notes that almost 80% of that generation considers patriotism a positive character trait with almost seventy percent thinking the same of honesty and intelligence. Negative traits are selfishness (about seventy percent) and sixty-three percent of that generation surveyed described the typical American as "lazy," another negative trait. Confidence in politics and political parties has also eroded significantly, with only about thirty percent expressing "confidence in the political wisdom of the American people." This generation believes that ordinary people are markedly superior at problem solving with more than seventy percent stating that regular citizens could do better solving our nation's problems than politicians.

On the religions aspects of life, only fifty-five percent of those surveyed view religious organizations as having a "positive effect on the way things are going in this country" with about twenty-five percent stating the same about national media. At the same time, this generation views small business, higher education, and technology in a most positive manner. They place large corporations, the entertainment industry, and banks on the bottom rungs of effective or key institutions. Millennials are typically *less religious yet more spiritual* than previous generations. About fifty-two percent of this generation express an "absolute certain belief in God" with sixty-seven percent expressing a belief in heaven and fifty-six percent believing in hell. What is most interesting about this data is its comparison to the "greatest generation" described by Tom Brokaw who coined the phrase to denote those born between about 1900 and 1927; who came of age during the Great Depression; and who fought World War II. Among that generation sixty-six percent expressed an absolute belief in God; sixty-nine percent believe in heaven; but only fifty percent believing in hell. And while the reduction from sixty-six percent to fifty-two percent on the question of an absolute belief in God appears significant, it is not markedly so and contrast with the essential parallel belief in heaven and the minor increase in the belief in hell among those born after 1980.

Millennials do not profess traditional religious beliefs, yet they are more likely than previous generations such as the "greatest generation" and "baby boomers" to engage in spiritual practices and endeavors. They profess a deep sense of wonder about the nature and workings of the universe, and note that they ponder the meaning and purpose of life at least on a weekly basis. This generation further expresses a strong sense of gratitude for what the world has offered them that is accompanied by a deep, abiding desire for of spiritual peace and well-being. Essentially, then, the differences between traditional senses of spirituality, religious belief, and gratitude between millennials and the 'greatest generation" are not that profound. This, then, may be the key to Masonic revitalization: what was the Craft doing immediately after World War II that attracted so many like-minded men? The answer appears simple: the Craft looked to its past and observed what didn't work (see demise of the Odd Fellows as an example), contrasted it with what did work (the emergence and vitalization of Freemasonry world-wide in the eighteenth and nineteenth centuries), and learned. George Santayana's admonition that those who do not remember the past are condemned to repeat it is two pronged. Yes, we need to learn from our mistakes, but we also need to learn from our successes and, even, revitalize that which has been discarded when we discover that its replacement is not bearing fruit.

So how does Freemasonry proceed to revitalize itself and appeal to a prime target for membership—millennials. Andrew Hammer in his book *Observing the Craft* as well in the seminars he gives nationally has a range of sound, valid recommendations that any Lodge can easily follow. The future of Freemasonry lies in its relationship with those born after 1980. This generation is significantly better educated than previous ones, and tends to ask pointed questions and seek clarity in its endeavors. They do not appreciate hearing excuses and demand accountability. But, as noted above, they are seeking the same things that the generation that proceeded World War II sought: spirituality, fulfillment, and meaning. It therefore behooves Freemasonry to address their concerns and desires. First and foremost, Freemasonry must clearly define itself.

Clarity is essential in all definitions. Freemasonry is not a religion and was never intended to be one nor to replace any religious tradition. It is a "system of moral instruction" which directly addresses man's search for meaning. It is a multi-layered presentation of the ultimate in meaning and moral behavior. Our ritual from its inception pointed clearly to the direct interconnection between man and the universe as well as his relationship to an intelligence greater than himself— "The Supreme Architect of the Universe." The Deists who made profound contributions to the Craft in its formative years referred to "The Deity" rather than to God. The millennial generation seeks spiritual clarification and direction in a similar manner. Freemasonry provides a uniquely creative organization for the expression— through ritual—of insights into the fundamental nature of man.

Freemasonry exists in two planes: visible (external) and invisible (internal). Its rituals and external expressions and structures are designed to fulfill the human need for external contact and validation while, at the same time, meeting the normal human urge to seek internal understanding and inspiration. The Craft exists to fulfill both the institutional function of giving expression to internal yearnings and to give insight into the significance of human existence. The Craft must recover its traditional center by utilizing our ritual to demonstrate the migration or journey from the visible and tactile to the invisible and spiritual. We are not a religion, but we enjoy a deep and vast sea of symbols, allegories, and philosophies without which our quest would make little sense. We must resurrect our focus on wisdom, on how we understand nature, and our relationship to it. We must study our traditions and history, not the myths and fables, and strengthen in new Masons a deep understanding of meaning. And finally, again through our ritual, we must create a beautiful, memorable experience for all Brethren.

At the same time, we must not consider tradition as tantamount to perfection and therefore something to be unquestioned or unchanged. Tradition has its place, especially in ritual, and links us with our past. But slavish adherence to tradition for tradition's sake alone can lead to disaster. In World War I, tradition taught the utilization of mass force along a front as well as siege tactics. This resulted in over four years of brutal, bloody trench stalemate on the Western Front which was not broken until mobility using tanks and airplanes was introduced as a tactic in 1917. At the end of the war, however, traditional military thinking prevailed, airpower was reduced and its impact, for a time, downgraded. Static defenses like the Maginot Line were established and deemed impregnable. The events of 1939, 1940, and 1941 quickly proved the tradition wrong. For the United States, the same error was made in Vietnam. Military tactics were based in the traditions of open plain tank warfare prevalent in Europe in the 1940s and little consideration was given to small, mobile unit tactics or guerrilla warfare. Tradition is a powerful force and is psychologically satisfying, but it must not be allowed to stifle necessary modifications and progress.

"One element that distinguished Freemasonry from almost all other social groups . . . with the exception of organized religious services is ritual"[4] notes the Social Issues Research Center in its report. Ritual, the report suggests, is often deemed an ancient relic or even simple superstition. It is neither. Ritual, as noted in previous chapters, is an essential element in human life and cultural continuity. Herbert Blumer in both the 1930s and the 1960s placed emphasis on human beings forming or defining their actions with their responses or reactions based upon interpretation. The focus is on the meaning of the behavior, not the act itself. Ritual exists in virtually every aspect of daily social behavior. Its ubiquity is self-evident. The questions for Freemasons, suggests the Social Issues Research Institute report, are of what import are Masonic rituals? Why do they exist? And what purpose do they serve? The General Secretary of the United Grand Lodge writes that "The ceremonial side is really one of our great differentiators, but . . . they are just plays . . . they are parables [and} . . . they are completely open to the public. You can have copies of them. You can go across the road and buy them. There's nothing secret about them."[5] Secret or not, the allegories contained in our rituals and the great moral lessons there inculcated are available in virtually no other place.

Masonic rituals are and always have been initiation rites which in traditional societies marked the transition into manhood. Among the younger Freemasons surveyed both in the U.G.L.E. commissioned study and others, the view expounded about ritual is that it holds a distinct attraction because it provides a sense of formality in an otherwise informal world. And Masonic ritual holds a further attraction to these more spiritually-oriented men in that the allegories enacted provide moral instruction based on sound ethical principles. To properly engage in ritual, though, requires an educated or inquisitive mind that seeks the underlying meaning of the actions and words to explain the moral code inculcated. The act of rote memorization required in good ritualization enables those involved to engage in the activity with a more profound sense of confidence and, once the words have been successfully "committed to heart," the opportunity presents itself to seek deeper meaning and self-actualization.

Masonic ritual did not spring forth full formed and complete. There are virtually no records of its creation, no authors' notes. There are still in existence numerous eighteenth century exposes, mainly of French origin, which claim to provide accurate accounts of Masonic ceremonies, but they are of dubious authorship Yet, as Alain Bernheim notes in *Masonic Catechisms and Exposures*, "Most scholars are now agreed that early manuscript catechisms and some of the printed ones provide fairly reliable information about masonic ceremonies of their time."[6] He further suggests that these printed documents indicate that Masonic ritual was transmitted "mouth to ear" but that some Brothers, fearing that they were deficient in memorization, put them in writing even though that violated their obligation. They do, however provide some insight into the development of the Fraternity's ritual during the eighteenth century and, the English Masonic exposes *Masonry Dissected* (1730), *Three Distinct Knocks* (1760), and *Jachin and Boaz* (1762) "show a certain development having taken place"[7] in British Freemasonry, as well. Similarly, Webb's 1818 *Monitor* and Duncan's 1866 *Ritual* demonstrate the development of Masonic ritual in the United States.

Early Lodges, as did craft lodges, performed a single ceremony and, as noted above, that evolved into a two and then three-degree system for instruction. The beginnings of Freemasonry are soundly set in progressive individualism and a search for moral authority. The rituals of Freemasonry, notes Hoffmann, "enabled Masonic ideas about moral and political order to be experienced on a physical level." [8] They provided an internal constitution that could direct the life of a person. Early Freemasonry viewed itself as a corrective institution in an ever-changing world by using the symbols of stone masonry to project a method for the transformation of personal life. Morality was to be as much internal as it was to be external. Inward civility became paramount and Freemasonry, solidly founded on a communal experience, followed the principle that externalization of the internal experience was essential if the Masonic value system was to be reinforced and incorporated into public life. And this was done through ritual.

The most significant question that seems to confront Freemasonry in the twenty-first century is how to proceed? What path to take? It is the apparent simplicity of the message, notes De Bias, that is misleading. Yet, as in the life of the medieval monk, the initiation ceremony was merely the beginning. He was then expected to embark on a life-long journey of reflection and analysis as well as learning and discussion. The simple dictums "love thy neighbor" or "know thyself" are fraught with problems, so too are Masonic allegories, symbols, and teaching. The various rituals may be likened to lighting a candle. It becomes the provenience of the Brother to utilize the light provided to find his path and fulfill his yearnings.

The first step in Craft enhancement (and some would suggest, survival) is to carefully "guard the west gate" and better vet or make a careful and critical examination of petitioners. Why is he interested in Freemasonry? Why did he elect to petition at this time? Why does he want to join? And not only what does he think Freemasonry has to offer him, but also what does he have to offer Freemasonry? Where did he gain his knowledge of Freemasonry? There is so much misinformation available, it is important to ask this question. It is also of importance to make sure that the petitioner understands fully the obligations he will incur once he becomes a member: moral, ethical, financial, time, and educational. More than one initiate has walked out of their first catechism class because they were not adequately instructed on what was expected and the level of commitment required.

The second step in this process is for the petitions committee and Lodge members to do due diligence by performing a thorough background check. There are numerous data bases available that provide a wealth of information about just about everyone. Does the petitioner have a Facebook page or twitter account, for example? A quick scan of newspaper archives will reveal if the petitioner has engaged in any public activity; is a member of other organizations; and his involvement in community affairs. The petitions committee should not fear asking pointed, difficult questions and expecting full and clear answers. Committee members should talk with neighbors, employers, and others in the community who might know the individual and know him well. Freemasonry is not a hereditary society and just because a candidate's father or any other ancestor was a Freemason does not automatically qualify him for membership. Members of the petitions' committee, in fact all Brothers, should ask themselves these questions: Would I employ this person and give him significant responsibility in my firm? Would I want to work with this person on a daily basis? Or, is this the kind of man I would want my daughter to marry and be happy to call son-in-law?

When the petitioner has been properly vetted, accepted, and initiated, the "real" work of the Craft begins: sound Masonic education. Freemasonry is a life-long pursuit and as such requires time, attention, and dedication. To demand that a Brother move through the degrees quickly does not match the declaration that it is a long quest. In the operative world, the apprentice could remain a "student" for seven years or more, and a fellow of the craft for life. Time is definitely a factor, however, and procrastination is not a sign of dedication or a desire to learn, but it may take some Brothers longer than others to master their catechisms. This can be paralleled with the military which regularly "recycles" recruits who do not master basic military skills. It is also paralleled in high education where the more diligent obtain a bachelor's degree in three years while others take six or more. Each Brother has his personal "cable tow" which should be used to determine his rate of progress, not some pre-determined time-frame. There are limits, yes, but overly fast advancement does not lead to an increase in retention or activity.

Essential to the advancement of all Brothers, not just degree candidates, is a sound mentoring program that goes far beyond the memorization of catechisms. A good Lodge does not desire indifferent or incomplete work. Mentoring throughout Masonic life provides the guidance essential to a fuller understanding of Freemasonry, its principles, its allegories, and its relationship to daily life. A Lodge mentor must be solidly grounded in Masonic history, philosophy, and allegories. He should be prepared to lead his students through the intricacies of the Craft and to answer their questions as fully as possible based on sound Masonic research and documentation. But even the most profound mentor is not all-knowing, there is no shame in stating "I don't know" and following that with "but I'll find out."

Tradition in Freemasonry is important, but it is not supreme. The *Book of Constitutions* states clearly that "preferment among Masons is grounded upon real worth and personal merit only." No one is guaranteed membership in a Masonic Lodge and once a member, no one is guaranteed any specific place in that Lodge or any other. If a Brother is unwilling to become proficient in the various rituals of the Craft; if he is unwilling to participate in the numerous Masonic education courses provided which give sound instruction in Masonic Law, Lodge management, and officer responsibilities; if he is unwilling to attend regularly; and if he is unwilling to demonstrate due respect to the Craft through proper decorum (see Chapter II); there is just cause to call into question his commitment to Freemasonry and his place in the Lodge other than on the side line.

Freemasonry is a fraternal organization not a business endeavor. But that does not mean that business practices have no place at the local or jurisdictional level. The Craft often uses the word "journey" to describe its activities, and as with any journey, plans must be made if the desired destination is to be reached. Just as a well-notated road map is necessary to the success of a protracted trip, so too is a well-developed strategic plan essential to the success of any organization, Masonic or otherwise. A strategic or long-range plan is not to be confused with the annual plan, though the annual plan may and should be representative of long-range goals. A long-range (five or ten or more years) plan should be visionary as well as directional. It should focus not only the current year's activities, but should project future initiatives.

A sound long-range plan begins with research to determine not only the current status of the organization, but also its vision, goals, objectives, and the strategies needed to implement them. These goals must, however, be compared realistically with current and past performance to determine if they are practical and within reach of the organization and include considerations of to what extent, if any, the organizations mission has changed in the recent past as well as why or why not changes occurred. It is virtually impossible to plan for the future without measuring and evaluating past successes and failures. Once the current position of the organization has been established, planning may begin.

The next step in establishing a solid long-range plan is to evaluate the organization's mission statement and principles. The mission statement should clearly state the purpose of the organization and how it plans to contribute directly to its constituency as well as to the larger world. A mission statement is a springboard, not an end result and may require restructuring as circumstances demand. Along with a mission statement should be a realistic view of the organization: its physical appearance to both internal and external audiences, its size, its activities, its budget, and, above all, its people. To use a craft analogy, without people, the machinery lays dormant and grows rusty; the buildings remain empty; and organizational goals go unfulfilled. The ultimate goal of any planning, long or short-ranged, is efficient and proper utilization of personnel and the permanent achievement of goals and objectives.

The United Grand Lodge of England has published its program "*The Future of Freemasonry*: Our Strategy 2015-2020" based upon the information provided by the Social Issues Research Center in 2012. It is obvious that local Lodges and, even, many Grand Lodges cannot afford such in-depth research, but that does not mean that they cannot perform their own research to help in developing both an annual and a long-range plan. The first step is probably best taken among the elected and appointed officers to determine their goals and expectations as well as their interests and their strengths. Next a local Lodge should survey its membership, formally or informally, to determine what talents are to be found among the Brothers and how those talents may best be put to use to further Masonic principles and practices. For example, not all Brothers are ritualists and many are not inclined toward such public performance, but these Brothers have a place in the Lodge be it in the dining area, assisting with charity, or simply supporting the Lodge and its officers in myriad ways. Other brothers are more comfortable as leaders and have the experience and temperament which marks them as such. And yet others serve best simply as spectators. Keep this in mind, the strength of most sporting events lies not in the players, but rather in the support of the spectators on the sidelines.

When the membership has been surveyed and its wishes, strengths, and suggestions considered, it is time to organize activities and the Lodge schedule. At the center of Masonic tradition is ritual and as such significant emphasis is properly placed on instruction and proficiency. Most Masonic Districts hold Schools of Instruction and some Lodges do so, as well. These schools provide in-depth instruction and practice in ritual. Most of the information contained in the preceding chapters focuses on the nature of ritual, its place in society, and its value to Freemasonry as a tool for transmitting our belief system and our meaning. It is the practice that so significantly marks Freemasonry as being exceptional. But additional Masonic education should not be neglected since it relates directly to our ritual as well as to our history, traditions, principles, and tenets. It is through sound Masonic education that the Brother achieves fulfillment in the Lodge.

At the same time, the charitable and civic activities of the Lodge must not be neglected, either. Freemasonry is not a fraternal benefit society, though charity is at the heart of our obligation. Nor is Freemasonry a strictly civic organization even though our traditions strongly support activities outside the Lodge and we encourage our Brothers to be good men who participate fully in civil society. We do, though, as individual Lodges, support a wide range of community activities to include scouting and other youth organizations; our various Masonic Youth groups; child ID programs; and a range of civic programs ranging from blood banks to shelters for abused children to recognizing educational endeavors, first responders, our military, and our veterans. We have also obligated ourselves to care for our poor and distressed which we do through activities including the Masonic Homes, forth-five of which are located in twenty states, as well as various medical and research centers. Each Lodge should determine for itself based on its analysis of its Brothers, the extent of its public and charitable activity.

To take the planning one step further, though, the local Lodge (and the Grand Lodge) is best served when strategies are put in place that support sound leadership and enhance membership involvement. Lodge governance is based in sound leadership and each Lodge should work diligently to develop new leaders and to retain proven ones. Each Lodge should also, within the limits of Masonic Law, investigate methods to attract new Brothers and to retain those initiated. A membership committee tasked to attract new members may be useful, but it is even more critical that a sound mentoring program be in place to ensure that all initiates are assigned a knowledgeable mentor who meets with them often and who is readily available for consultation.

A significant part of membership development depends upon local media coverage and the local Lodge may wish to establish a committee explicitly for that purpose. Coupled with this is the proper and efficient use of various electronic media outlets to make known to all Lodge activities and accomplishments. "Keeping one's light under a bushel" is not an effective way to let the world know of the greatness, dedication, and civic mindedness of our Brotherhood. And this type of positive publicity serves more than one purpose. We all desire to be on the "winning team," the team that is actively making positive contributions to its members and to society in general. And it is the winning team that receives the lion's share of publicity.

Finally, Masonic Lodges must accept the fact that they are a form of business and that this requires financial sustainability. It is essential that the Lodge does all possible to develop and maintain physical facilities which meet the expectations of the "modern man." Lodge property should be conserved properly and with that goes the identification and establishment of a steady income flow to ensure that the outward appearance of the Fraternity does not grow shabby. Likewise, internal appearance should also be addressed as noted under the section on decorum. The ultimate questions to be answered by every Lodge and Grand Lodge is "do we provide a quality experience for our Brothers? Do we fully meet his expectations?"

To meet the goals established at every level, it becomes incumbent that local Lodges and Grand Lodges introduce and follow through with some form of evaluation to determine what should be amended and what retained. It is also critical that even more rigorous leadership training be developed accompanied with a focus on that solidly Masonic tradition of virtually flawless ritual. Freemasonry, notes the Social Issues Research Center report, has at its root "moral precepts and modes of conduct that are far from being at odds with mainstream society."[9] The local Lodge has become a place of refuge, peace, and tranquility in a turbulent world. It has been, from its beginning, an example for civil society and organization through its encouragement of free discussion without censorship or authoritarianism. It also has within its realm of influence the opportunity to prove itself even more relevant in the present and coming age that it was in past ages. The state which once expanded to encompass so many traditionally civic activities seems now to have reached its limit and begun to contract. This provides an opportunity for Freemasonry to step from the "shadows" and regain its place as the preeminent Fraternity founded on brotherly love, relief, and truth. Social engineering comes not from government activity, but rather from the activities of men and women. It emerges from the type of strong bond that is established within Freemasonry which historically has rejected intolerance while encouraging human benevolence.

Men are attracted to Freemasonry, notes the results of the British study and confirmed by the Pew research, by the attraction of friendship and belonging. Freemasonry's altruism is also attractive, especially to millennials. It further offers sound tradition in what is quickly becoming a world void of tradition and our ritual offers comfort in times of trouble at the personal, community, and national levels. Freemasonry must look closer at its past and its rituals if it is to be successful in the present and the future, and if it is to remain true to the traditions of the Craft.

NOTES

1. H.B. Nisbet. *Lessing: Philosophical and Theological Writings.* (Cambridge, UK: Cambridge University Press, 2005), 189.

2. Nisbet. *Lessing: Philosophical and Theological Writings,* 190-205

3. "The Future of Freemasonry: A Report of by the Social Issues Research Centre 2012," 24.

4. "The Future of Freemasonry," 25.

5. "The Future of Freemasonry," 30.

6. Alain Bernheim. *Masonic Catechisms and Exposures.* Located at http://www.fremasons-freemasonry.com/bernheim 8.html, p. 1. Retrieved 11 February 2016.

7. Bernheim, *Masonic Catechisms,* 2.

8. S.L. Hoffmann, *The Politics of Sociability Freemasonry and German Civil Society 1840-1918.* Translated by Tom Lampert. Ann Arbor, MI: University of Michigan Press, 2007, p. 8.

9. "The Future of Freemasonry, 35.

Bibliography

Alberge, Dalya. "Stones May Have Been First Erected in Wales, Evidence Suggests." At http:theguardian.com/un-news/2015/dec/or/stonehenge-first-erected-in-wales.

Allen, Reginald E. (ed.). *Greek Philosophy: Thales to Aristotle, 3rd Edition, Revised and Expanded.* New York: The Free Press, 1991.

Anderson, James. *The Constitutions of Free-Masons: Containing the History, Charges, Regulations, of That Ancient and Right Worshipful Fraternity, for the Use of the Lodges, London, printed by W. Hunter, for J. Senex and J. Hooke in that Year Of Masonry 7523, Anno Domioni 1723.* New York: Masonic Publishers, 1855.

Anonymous. *The Graham Manuscript.* Abt. 1725. Located at www.omdhs.syracusemasons.com/sites/default/files/philosophy/Graham%20ms%20-%208%20pt%20copy.pdf, retrieve January 9, 2016.

———. *Jachin and Boaz or an Authentic Key to the Door of Free-Masonry.* London: Printed for Nichol at the Paper Mill, 1763. Reprint. Kessinger Publishing, 2012.

———. *Three Distinct Knocks.* London: Printed by H. Srjeant, 1760. Reprint. Kessinger Publishing, 2012.

Aristotle. *Nicomachean Ethics* at http://classics.mit.edu/Aristotle/nicomachaen.html, retrieved September 1, 2015

Ashmole, Elias. *Memories of the Life of the Life of the Learned Antiquary Elias Ashmole, Esq: Drawn up by Himself by Way of Diary: With an Appendix of Original Letters. Publish's by Charles Burman, Esq.* New York: ECCO Press, 2012.

Aungier, George James. *The History and Antiquities of Syon Monastery, the Parish of Isleworth and the Chapely of Hounslow.* London: J.B. Nichols and Sons, 1840.

Austin, Justin. *How to Do Things with Words.* Cambridge: Harvard University Press, 1962.

Barber, Malcolm. *The New Knighthood: A History of the Order of the Temple, 12th Edition.* Cambridge, UK: Cambridge University Press, 2015.

———. *The Trial of the Templars.* Cambridge, UK: Cambridge University Press, 2012. Barber, Malcolm, and Bate, Keith. *The Templars: Selected Resources.* Manchester, UK: Manchester University Press, 2002.

Beadle, Richard and Fletcher, Alan (eds.). *The Cambridge Companion to Medieval English Theatre, 2nd Ed.* London: Cambridge University Press, 2008.

Beadle, Richard, and King Pamela (eds.). *York Mystery Plays: A Selection in Modern Spelling.* New York: Oxford University Press, 1995.

Beck, Guy L. "Celestial Lodge Above: The Temple of Solomon in Jerusalem as a Religious Symbol in Freemasonry." *Nova Religio: The Journal of Alternative and Emergent Religions, Vol. 4 No. 1* (2000), pp. 28-51.

Bell, Catherine. *Ritual: Perspectives and Dimensions.* New York: Oxford University Press, 1997.

———. *Ritual Theory: Ritual Practice.* New York: Oxford University Press, 1992.

———. *Teaching Ritual.* New York: Oxford University Press, 2007.

Bernheim, Alain. *Masonc Catechisms and Exposures.* Pietre-Stones Review of Freemasonry, Located at http://www.freemasons-freemasonry.com/bernheim8.html. Retrieved 11 February 2016.

Bevington, David. *Medieval Drama.* Boston: Houghton Company, 1975.

Bizzack, John. *For the Good of the Order: Examining the Shifting Paradigm within Freemasonry.* Pittsburg, PA: Autumn House Publishing, 2013.

Bogdan, Henrik. *Western Esotericism and Rituals of Initiation.* Albany: University of New York Press, 2007.

Bogdan, Henrik, and Snoek, Jan (eds.). *Handbook of Freemasonry.* Boston: Brill, 2014.

Boulton, Marjorie. *The Anatomy of Drama.* London: Routledge and Kegan Paul, 1971.

"Brideshead Revisited" at http://www.springfieldspringfield.co.uk/movie_script.php?movie=brideshead-revisited.

Bradley, Richard. *Ritual and Domestic Life in Prehistoric Europe.* London: Rutledge, 2005.

Brockett, Oscar, and Hildy, Franklin. *History of the Theatre, Tenth Edition.* New York: Pearson, 2007.

Bruner, Jerome. *Making Stories: Law, Literature, and Life.* Cambridge, MA: Harvard University Press, 202.

Bullock, Steven G. "A Pure and Sublime System: The Appeal of Post-Revolutionary Freemasonry." *Journal of the Early Republic, Vol. 9* (1989): pp. 359-373.

Burkert, Walter. *Ancient Mystery Cults.* Cambridge, Mass.: Oxford University Press, 1987.

Burkle, William S. "A Guide for the New Esoteric Freemason." At Pietre-Stones; Review of Freemasonry, http://www.freemasons/freemsonry.com/esoteric-freemason.html. Retrieved January 5, 2016.

Campbell, Joseph with Moyers, Bill. *The Power of Myth.* New York: Anchor Books, 1988.

Carnes, Mark. C. *Secret Ritual and Manhood in Victorian America.* New Haven: Yale University Press, 1989.

Carr, Harry (ed.). *The Early Masonic Catechisms.* Kila, MT: Kessinger Publishing Company, undated.

———. *The Early Masonic Catechisms Transcribed and Edited by Douglas Knoop, M.A., G.P. Jones, M.A. and Douglas Hamer, M.A.* London: Manchester University Press, 1963.

———. *Three Distinct Knocks and Jachin and Boaz with an Introduction and Commentaryby Harry Carr.* Bloomington, IL: The Masonic Book Club, 1981

Cassirer, Ernst. *The Philosophy of Symbolic Forms.* Chicago: Open Court Publishing, 1923.

"Character of a Freemason" in *A Farmer's Almanac,* Andover, Mass., 1823.

Churton, Tobias. *The Magus of Freemasonry: The Mysterious Life of Elias Ashmole—Scientist, Alchemist, and Founder of the Royal Society.* Rochester Vermont: Inner Traditions, 2006.

Coil, Henry W. *Coil's Masonic Encyclopedia.* New York: Macoy Publishing & Masonic Supply, Inc., 1991.

Condor, Edward. *Records of the Hole Crafte and Fellowship of Masons: With a Chronicle of the History of the Worshipful Company of Masons of the City of London; Collected from Official Records in the Possession of the Company, the Manuscripts in the British Museum, the Public Record Office, the Guildhall Library, Etc. Et.* London: Swan, Sonnenschein & Company, 1894.

Coldewey, John (ed.). *Early English Drama: An Anthology.* New York: Garland Reference Library of the Humanities, 1993.

Cua, Antonia. *Human Nature, Ritual and History: Studies in Xanzi and Chinese Philosophy.* New York: The Catholic University Press. 2005.

Da Costa, Helio L. Jr. *The Chamber of Reflection.* Located at http://freemasonry.bcy.ca/Texts/gmd1991/pondering.html. Retrieved, October 15, 2015.

Davis, Robert. *The Mason's Word: The History and Evolution of the American Masonic Ritual.* Guthrie, OK: Building Stone Publishing, 2013.

————. *Understanding Manhood in America: Freemasonry's Enduring Path to the Mature Masculine.* Lancaster, VA: Anchor Communication LLC, 2005

De Bias, Jean-Louis. *Secrets and Practices of the Freemasons: Sacred Mysteries, Rituals, And Symbols Revealed.* Woodbury, MN: Llewellyn Publications, 2013.

De Hoyos, Arturo. *Light on Masonry: The History and Rituals of America's Most Important Masonic Expose.* Washington, DC: Scottish Rite Research Society, 2008.

Drake, Nadia. "Neanderthals Built Mysterious Stone Circles," in *National Geographic,* May, 2016, located at http://news.nationalgeographic.com/2016/05/neanderthals-caves-rings-building-archeology.

Driver, Tom. *Liberating Rites: Understanding the Transformative Power of Ritual.* Boulder, CO: Westview, 1998.

Duncan, Hugh. *Symbols in Society.* New York: Oxford University Press, 1968.

Duncan, Malcolm. *Duncan's Masonic Ritual and Monitor or Guide to the Three Symbolic Degrees of the Ancient York Rite and to the Degrees of Mark Master, Past Master, Most Excellent Master, and the Royal Arch.* 1866. Reprint. New York: Crown Publishers, 2008.

Durkheim, Emile. *The Elementary Forms of Religious Life.* New York: Free Press, 1995.

"Early Masonic Manuscripts." Located at http://www.rgle.org.uk/RGLE_Old_Charges-htm.

Ecco, Umberto. *The Name of the Rose.* New York: Harcourt, 1983.

Elliott, Paul, and Daniels, Stephen. "The 'School of True, Useful and Universal Science'? Freemasonry, Natural Philosophy and Scientific Culture in Eighteenth-Century England." *BJHS Vol. 39 No. 2* (2006): pp. 207-229.

"English Royal Freemasons" located at www.freemasonry.london.museum.

Enns, Peter. *Exodus: The NIV Application Commentary.* New York: Zondervan, an imprint of Harper Collins, 2000.

"Famous American Freemasons" located at http://phoenixmasonry.org/famous_masons.htm.

Faivre, Antoine. *Access to Western Esotericism.* Albany, NY: State University of New York Press, 1994.

Frazer, James. *The Golden Bough: A Study of Magic and Religion.* New York: Cosimo, 2009.

Fried, Albert and Elman, Richard (eds.) *Charles Booth's London.* London: Hutchinson, 1969.

Gassner, John. *Medevial and Tudor Drama.* New York: Applause Books, 1993.

Gelber, Steven M., and Cook, Martin L. *Saving the Earth: A History of a Middle-Class Millenarian Movement.* Berkley: University of California Press, 1990.

Gertz, Clifford. *The Interpretations of Cultures: Selected Essays by Clifford Gertz.* New York: Basic Books, 1973.

————. (ed). *Myth, Symbol and Culture.* New York: W.W. Norton & Company, Inc., 1971.

Goodrick-Clarke, Nicholas. *The Western Exoteric Traditions.* New York: Oxford University Press, 2008.

Gould, Robert. *A Concise History of Freemasonry.* New York: Macoy Publishing, Co., 1904.

Gould, Robert and Freke, Robert. *A Concise History of Freemasonry.* New York: CreateSpace Independent Publishing Platform, 2013.

————. *The History of Freemasonry: Its Antiquities, Symbols, Constitution, Customs, Etc.* London: Thomas C. Jack, 1885.

Gregor, Thomas. "Far, Far Away My Shadow Wandered." *American Ethnologist 9* (1991): pp.709-720.

Grimes, Ronald L. *Rites out of Place.* New York: Oxford University Press, 2006.

————. *Ritual Criticism: Case Studies in Its Practice, Essays on Its Theory.* Columbia, SC: University of South Carolina Press, 1990.

Grossman, Cathy. "Survey '72% of Millennials' more spiritual than religious." USA Today, August 27, 2010.

Gunn, Joshua. "Death by Publicity: U.S. Freemasonry and the Public Drama of Secrecy." *Rhetoric & Public Affairs Vol. 11 No. 2* (2008): pp. 243-278.

Hamill, John. *The Craft.* London: Crucible, 1986.

Hamill, John and Gilbert, Robert (eds.). *Freemasonry: A Celebration of the Craft.* North Dighton, MA: J.G. Press, 1993.

Hammer, Andrew. *Observing the Craft: The Pursuit of Excellence in Masonic Labor and Observance.* Mindhive Books.com, 2010.

Happe, Peter, (ed.). *English Mystery Plays.* Harmondworth, UK: Penguin Books, 1975.

Hayakawa, S.I. *Language as Thought and Action.* New York: Harcourt Brace, 1952.

Hendon, Ted. H. "Of Freemasons, Odd Fellows, and Passenger Pigeons." *Masonic Messenger: Official Publication of the Grand Lodge of Georgia, F. & A.M.,* January 1992, pp. 13-14.

Hextall, W.B. *The Hiramic Legend and The Ashmolean Theory.* Derbyshire, UK: Self -Published, not dated.

Higgins, Frank. *The Beginning of Masonry.* New York; Self-published, 1916.

Hodapp, Christopher. *Freemasons for Dummies.* New York: John Wiley & Sons Inc., 2013.

Hobsbawm, Eric, and Ranger, Terrance (eds.). *The Invention of Tradition.* New York: Routledge, 1996.

Hoffmann, S.I. *The Politics of Sociability Freemasonry and German Civil Society 1840-1918.* Translated by Tom Lampert. Ann Arbor, MI: University of Michigan Press, 2007.

Hogan, Timothy. *The Alchemical Keys to Masonic Ritual.* Self-published, wwwllulu.com, 2007.

Hubert, Henri, and Mauss, Marcel. *Sacrifice: Its Nature and Function.* Chicago: University of Chicago Press, 1964.

Huxley, Julian (ed.). "A Discussion on Ritualization Behavior in Animals and Man" in *Philosophical Transactions of the Royal Society,* series B, 251, 1966.

Johnson, Melvin. *Freemasonry in American Prior to 1750: Being an Address by Most Worshipful Melvin Maynard Johnson Grand Master to the Grand Lodge of Massachusetts.* Cambridge, Mass.: Caustic-Claflin Company, 1917.

Jung, C.G. and Jaffee, Aniela. *Memories, Dreams, Reflections.* New York: Knopf Doubleday, 1965.

Karg, Barb, and Young, John. *100 Secrets of the Freemasons: The Truth Behind the World's Most Mysterious Society.* Avon, Massachusetts: Adams Media, 2009

Karpiel, Frank J. Jr. "Mystic Ties of Brotherhood: Freemasonry, Ritual, and Hawaiian Royalty in the Nineteenth Century." *Pacific Historical Review Vol. 69 No. 3* (2000): pp. 357-397.

Knoop, Douglas and Jones, G.P. *A Short History of Freemasonry to 1730.* London: Manchester University Press, 1940.

———. *An Introduction to Freemasonry.* London: Manchester University Press, 1937.

———. *The Evolution of Masonic Organizations.* Manchester, UK: Manchester University, 1932.

———. *The Genesis of Freemasonry: An Account of the Rise and Development of Freemasonry in Its Operative, Accepted, and Early Speculative Phases.* Manchester, UK; Manchester University Press, 1949.

———. *The London Mason in the Seventeenth Century.* Manchester, UK: Manchester University Press, 1935.

———. *The London Freemasons in the Seventeenth Century.* Manchester, UK: Manchester University Press, 1935.

———. *The Mediaeval Mason.* Manchester, UK: Manchester University Press, 1933.

Kolko-Rivera, Mark. *Freemasonry: An Introduction.* New York: Penguin Group, 2007.

Kosselleck, Reinhart, *Critique and Crisis: Enlightenment and the Pathogenesis of Modern Society* (Oxford, UK: Berg, 1988).

Kostof, Spiro. *A History of Architecture: Settings and Rituals Second Edition.* New York: Oxford University Press, 1995.

Lakoff, George, and Johnson, Mark. *Metaphors We Live By.* Chicago: University of Chicago Press, 1980.

Lang, Andrew. *Myth, Ritual, and Religion, Volume 1.* London: Longmans, Green and Company, 1887.

Langer, Susanne. *Philosophy in a New Key.* Cambridge: Harvard University Press, 1942.

———. *Mind: An Essay on Human Feelings.* 3 Vols. Baltimore: Johns Hopkins University Press 1982.

Little Masonic Library, 5 Vols. Richmond, Virginia: Macoy Publishing, 1977.

Littlejohn, Stephen. *Theories of Human Communication.* Columbus, Ohio: Charles E. Merrill Publishing Company, 1978.

Littlejohn, Stephen, and Foss, Karen. *Theories of Human Communication, Ninth Edition.* New York: Wadsworth, 2008.

Mackey, Albert. *The History of Freemasonry V Volumes.* New York: The Masonic History Company, 1898.

Mackey, Albert and Singleton, William. *The French Masonic Guilds in the Middle Ages.* New York: Kessinger Publishing and Legacy Press, 2012.

MacNulty, W. Kirk. *Freemasonry: Symbols, Secrets, Significance.* London: Thames & Hudson Ltd., 2006.

Marshall, Douglas A. "Behavior, Belonging, and Belief: A Theory of Ritual Practice." *Social Theory Vol. 20 No. 3* (2002): 360-380.

McLaren, Peter L. "Rethinking Ritual." *ETC: A Review of General Semantics Vol. 41 No. 3* (1984): 267-277.

Martin, Sean. *The Knights Templar: The History and Myth of the Legendary Order.* New York: Basic Books, 2009.

McClendon, Charles. *The Origins of Medieval Architecture: Building Europe, A.D. 600-900.* New Haven, Conn.: Yale University Press, 2005.

Meade, George. *Mind, Self and Society.* Chicago: The University of Chicago Press, 1934.

Melzer, Arthur. *Philosophy between the Lines.* Chicago: The University of Chicago Press, 2014.

Millar, Angel. *Freemasonry: A History.* San Diego, CA: Thunder Bay Press, 2005.

Moore, Charles. *The New Masonic Trestle-Board: Adapted to the Work and Lectures as Practiced in Lodges, Chapters, Councils, and Encampments of Knights Templars, in the United States of America.* 1868. Reprint. London: Forgotten Books, 2012.

"Mortem Obire – Confronting Death: The Poetics of Silence, Light, Healing, and Truth in Architecture" at http://ritualarchitecture.blogspot.com retrieved 22 January 2016.

Newman, Sharan. *The Real History Behind the Templars.* Berkley, CA: Berkley Trade Publishing, 2007.

Newton, Joseph. *The Builders: A Story and Study of Masonry.* New York: George H. Doran, Co., 1914.

Nicholson, Helen. *The Knights Templar: A New History.* Gloucestershire, UK: The History Press, 2010.

Nisbet, H.B. *Lessing: Philosophical and Theological Writings.* Cambridge, UK: Cambridge University Press, 2005.

Normington, Katie. *Medieval English Drama.* Malden, MA: Polity Press, 2009.

Nowell, Alan. "Dance Traces in the Ritual of Freemasonry." *Archeology of Ireland Vol. 24 No. 1* (2010): pp. 26-30.

Odiorne, James. *Opinions on Speculative Masonry, Relative to Its Origin, Nature, and Tendency.* Boston: Perkins & Marvin, 1830.

Perkins, Sij. "Mysterious Underground Rings Built by Neanderthals," *Science Magazine,* May, 2016, located at http://www.sciencemag.org/news/2016/05/mysterious-undergroundrings-built-neandertals.

Perreault, Charles, and Mathew, Sarah. "Dating the Origin of Language Using Phonermic Diversity," PLOS/ONE, April 27, 2012, located at http://journals.plos.org/plosone/article?id=10.1371/journal.pone.0035289.

Pew Research Center. "A Portrait of 'Generation Next: How Young People View Their Lives, Futures and Politics." Located at http://www.people-press.org/2007/01/09/a-portrait-of-geneartion-next.htm, January 9, 2007.

Plot., Robert. *A Natural History of Strafford-Shire by Robert Plot, 1686.* London: Printed at the Theatre, 1686.

Poll, Michael (ed.) *Ancient Manuscripts of Freemason: The Transformation from Operative to Speculative Freemasonry.* New Orleans: Cornerstone Books, 2013.

————. *Masonic Enlightenment: The Philosophy, History and Wisdom of Freemasonry.* Lafayette, LA: Cornerstone Book Publishers, 2006.

Prescott, Andrew. *A History of British Freemasonry 1425-2000.* Sheffield, UK: Centre for Research into Freemasonry and Fraternalism (CRFF) at the University of Sheffield, 2001.

Preston, William. *Preston's Masonry.* 1779. Reprint. Kerssinger Legacy Reprints, 2014.

————. *Illustrations of Masonry William Preston.* 1861. Reprint. London: Forgotten Books, 2013.

Pritchard, Samuel. *Masonry Dissected.* New York: Poemandres Press Masonic Publishers, 1996.

Proceedings of the National Masonic Convention: Held at Baltimore, Maryland, May, A.L. 5853—A.D. 1843. Baltimore: Joseph Robinson, 1843.

Propp, Vladimir. *Morphology of the Folktale.* Austin, TX: University of Texas Press, 1968.

Ralls, Karen. *Knights Templar Encyclopedia.* Wayne, NJ: New Page Books, 2007.

Rappaport, Roy. *Ritual and Religion in the Making of Humanity.* New York: Cambridge University Press, 1999.

Rebold, Emmanuel and Brennan, J. Fletcher. *Primitive Masonic Laws and Charters (Extracted From General History of Freemasonry in Europe Based Upon the Ancient Documents Relating to and the Monuments Erected by This Fraternity from its Foundation in the Year 715 BC and the Present Time.* 1867. Reprint, New York: Kessinger Publishing, 2014.

"Redefining the Sacred: Religious Identity, Ritual Practices, and Sacred Architecture in the Near East and Egypt, 1000BC – AD 300." Located at http://www.orinst.ox.ac.uk/conferences/redefining_the_sacred/abstracts./html, retrieved January 22, 2016.

Robinson, John. *Born in Blood: The Lost Secrets of Freemasonry.* New York: M. Evans, 1989.

Schechner, Richard. *Between Theatre and Anthropology.* Philadelphia: University of Pennsylvania Press, 1985.

————. *Performance Theory.* New York: Routledge, 2003.

————. *Ritual, Play and Performance.* New York: The Seabury Press, 1977.

————. "Performers and Spectators Transported and Transformed." *Kenyon Review, Vol. III No.4,* pp. 83-113, 1981.

Schmidt, Leigh Eric. "From Arbor Day to the Environmental Sabbath: Nature, Liturgy, and American Protestantism." *Harvard Theological Review, 84, No. 3,* pp. 299-323, 1991.

Scott, Leader. *The Cathedral Builders: The Story of a Great Masonic Guild.* New Orleans: Cornerstone Book Publishers, 2013

Seaquist, Carl. "Ritual Individation and Ritual Change." *Method and Study of Religion Vo. 21* (2009): pp. 340-360.

Segal, Robert. "The Myth-Ritualist Theory of Religion," in *Journal for the Scientific Study of Religion, 19, No. 2,* 1980.

Sontag, Susan. *Illness as Metaphor.* New York: Doubleday, 1990.

Steiner, Rudolf. *Freemasonry and Ritual Work: The Collected Works of Rudolf Steiner.* Great Barrington, Mass.: Steiner Books, 2007.

Steinmetz, George. *The Lost Word, Its Hidden Meaning: A Correlation of the Allegory and Symbolism of the Bible with that of Freemasonry and the Exposition of the Secret Doctrine.* New York: Mccoy Publishing, 1953.

Stephenson, Barry. *Ritual: A Very Short Introduction.* New York: Oxford University Press, 2015.

The Dartmouth Bible. Boston: Houghton Mifflin Company, 1961.

"The Future of Freemasonry: A Report by the Social Issues Research Center 2012." Commissioned by the United Grand Lodge of England, published March 2012.

The Oxford Annotated Bible. New York: Oxford University Press, 1962.

Thorpe, Lewis. *Geoffrey of Monmouth, History of the Kings of Britain.* London: Guild Publishing, 1966.

Turner, Victor. *From Ritual to Theatre: The Human Seriousness of Play.* New York: PAJ Publications, 1982.

————. *The Forests of Symbols.* Ithaca, NY: Cornell University Press, 1967.

————. *The Ritual Process: Structure and Anti-Structure.* New Brunswick, Conn.: Aldine Transaction, 2008.

Twersky, Isadore, (ed.). "Mishneh Torah Book 1" in *A Maimonides Reader.* New York: Behrman House, 1972.

Upton-Ward, J.M. *The Rule of the Templars.* Woodbridge, Suffolk: The Boydell Press, 1992.

Urban, Hugh B. "Elitism and Esotericism: Strategies of Secrecy and Power in South Indian Tantra and French Freemasonry. *NUMEN Vol. 44* (1997): pp. 1-38.

Vibert, Lionel. *Freemasonry before the Existence of Grand Lodges.* London: Spencer & Co., Not dated.

Waddy, Van. "The Grail Legend by Emma Jung and Marie-Louise Franz." *Jung Society of America, Winter 2002,* pp. 12-14.

Webb, Thomas. *The Freemason's Monitor or Illustrations of Freemasonry.* 1802, Reprint. Kessinger Legacy Reprints, 2015.

Weisman, S. Gilbert. *Grand Oration, Grand Lodge of Florida, May 2015.* Located at http://grandlodgefl.com/archive_2014/grand_oration_2014.html.

Wiles, David. "Hrotsvitha of Gandersheim: The Performance of Her Plays in the Tenth Century." *Theatre History Studies 19,* June 1999, pp. 133-150.

———. *A Short History of Western Performance Space.* Cambridge, UK: Cambridge University Press, 2003.

Wilmhurst, Walter L. *Meaning of Masonry.* Sioux Falls, SD: NuVision Publications, 2007, originally published in 1927.

———. *The Relation of Masonry to the Ancient Mysteries Extracted from The Meaning of Masonry.* New York: Kessinger Publishing and Legacy Press, 2012.

Index

About the Author

Dr. Oscar Patterson III will be installed as Worshipful Master of Ashlar Lodge No. 98 Free and Accepted Masons in St. Augustine, Florida, Grand Lodge of Florida, on December 27, 2016. He holds the Gold Proficiency ard and is State Chairman for Public Education and Citizenship. He is also a member of the York Rite and Scottish Rite to include the York Rite College, Allied Masonic Degrees, and Red Cross of Constantine as well as The Masonic Society, The Philalethes Society, and Quatuor Coronati Lodge No. 2076's Correspondence Circle and several research Lodges in the United States. His Masonic research has appeared in Masonic journals and magazines in the United States and the United Kingdom.

Patterson holds the B.A. in religion and philosophy, the M.F.A. in design, and the Ph.D. in Communication Theory and Research. He is now retired but served as a professor and administrator at several universities in the U.S. during his thirty-five-year teaching career. He also lectured at universities in Europe, and South America as well as the United States, and was appointed as a Fulbright Fellow. His scholarly articles appeared in major academic journals and he has presented papers at numerous conferences.

Prior to beginning his academic career, Patterson was a Methodist minister, a juvenile officer, and an infantry officer with command and staff assignments in Vietnam. He also spent time as an actor and theatrical designer. He is a native of North Carolina who worked his way through college surveying land and in a textile mill. He lives in Ponte Vedra Beach, Florida, where he does administrative work as a volunteer for fifteen hours each week for the county sheriff.